REJOICE!

THE LORD
IS OUR
KEEPER

RECEIVED BY

Suzannah Fitzroy
&
Compiled and edited by
Russ Fitzroy

THE "KEEP" IN A CASTLE IS A STRONG TOWER.
IT IS THE SAFEST PLACE IN THE CASTLE,
AND IT IS THE LORD'S HOME!

"The Lord is your keeper;
The Lord is your shade on your right hand."
Psalm 121:5

Published by CSA Publishing
A department of Christian Services Association
P.O. Box 1017, Maricopa, Arizona 85139
www.XPpublishing.com

ISBN: 978-1-621660-69-9

**Printed in the United States of America
for Worldwide Distribution**

DEDICATION

TO FATHER GOD, WHO MADE US ONE

IN JESUS CHRIST, HIS ONLY SON,

THROUGH HIS HOLY SPIRIT'S POWER

WE DEDICATE OUR BOOK THIS HOUR.

HE GAVE US THE PRIVILEGE
OF LISTENING TO HIS VOICE;

WE KNOW, AT HIS FEET, YOU TOO
WILL MAKE HIM YOUR CHOICE.

FOREWORD

Suzannah does not consider herself to hold the "office of the prophet." However, as the apostle Paul said, "All may prophesy." She is gifted in the body of Christ as an exhorter, so we pray that these writings will be received as exhortation. These and all our writings are intended for the sole purpose of bringing glory and honor to our Lord and Savior, Jesus, the Christ, and to encourage and comfort His Bride, the Church. Suzannah believes she received these words directly from God, exclusively for His glorious Bride. Each person will receive something different, as there are many ways to receive from our Lord. Please allow Him, who is the Author and Finisher of our faith, to show you His particular path for your journey as you set yourself apart to be with Him.

Love in Jesus forever,

Russ
Husband, Editor, and Suzannah's Best Friend

We believe that all exhortation not recorded in the Bible must be weighed carefully and should be tested, using the Scripture as the standard, in order to hold onto what is good (1 Thessalonians 5:21).

PROMISED LAND

HIS SONG TO US

Come away My dove, My fair one,
and spend some time with Me,
Come away My dove, My fair one,
I long to set you free,
Come away My dove, My fair one,
I have much for you to see,
Come away My dove, My fair one,
and stay awhile with Me.
(Psalm 42:8; Zephaniah 3:17)

Over mountains and through valleys,
your path has often been;
Over hills and desert waste lands;
I've freed your soul from sin.
Never fear where I shall lead you,
for I hold you in My hand,
Come away My dove, My fair one,
into the promised land.
(Song of Solomon 4:1 & 8; Joshua 1)

Come away My dove, My fair one,
and spend some time with Me,
Come away My dove, My fair one,
I long to set you free,
Come away My dove, My fair one,
for I want you just to be;
Come away My dove, My fair one,
and rest awhile in Me.

My Darling, I do love you,
and I want the world to know,
That this retreat was planned by Me
because I love you so.
You know I'll never leave you;
your rest can be complete,
If you will come away with Me
and just sit at My feet.
(Hebrews 4) (Darling – one tenderly beloved)

Come away My dove, My fair one,
and spend more time with Me,
Come away My dove, My fair one,
you long to be set free,
Come away My dove, My fair one,
from out of bondage flee,
Come away My dove, My fair one,
forever reign with Me.

Drink deeply, My beloved.
Drink deeply of My love,
Come, let Me fill your being
with oceans from above.
Receive from Me, My sweet one,
the tenderness you need;
Remember I'm your Shepherd,
now from My pasture feed.
(Song of Solomon 8:14; Psalm 23)

Come away My dove, My fair one,
and spend this time with Me.

Prime the Pump

Our prayer is that you would use these words to "prime the pump" of your own worship and adoration of our Lord, Jesus Christ. Our hope is that this little book will be a jumping off point for you to have a deeper, more intimate and personal relationship with our Lord. Please consider seeking Him before you read these offerings, and then allow Him to minister the contents, through meditating upon the portions that He makes alive to your heart. Hopefully, these writings will be of use to enhance your desire to draw near to "The beauty and delightful loveliness of our Lord." Whether you use this as a page-a-day devotional, a chapter-a-month study, or however the Lord leads you, we pray that you will enjoy and rejoice with us in His wonderful manifest presence.

Forever yours in Jesus,
Russ and Suzi

A SPECIAL THANK YOU

A SPECIAL THANK YOU to My family and friends for their prayer, support, and encouragement:

First of all, to My faithful husband Russ for his dedication to the editing of this offering and others that will be coming your way very soon.

To My precious sister Maryanne Borden, and to My three wonderful daughters, Candy Fitzroy, Deborah Wuehler, and Heather Peake, for their constant love and joyful spirits.

To My dearest friends, Anna Helms and Pastor Karen McLaughlin-Brogan, for their heartfelt prayers and encouragement.

"But He answered, 'It is written, "Man shall not live by bread alone, but by every word that comes from the mouth of God" (Matthew 4:4).

INTRODUCTION

ABOVE THE TEMPORAL

I want you to put aside all of your concerns and cast off all of your worries onto My capable shoulders. My desire is that you would live in true freedom, just as a child, filled with My joy. You cannot do this as long as you hold onto the responsibilities that are not assigned to you. When you have taken burdens upon yourself to fix others, in your own strength and with your own understanding, then you block the flow of My Spirit's wisdom and intervention. I know your intentions are well meaning, but this is not your highest calling. Don't settle for mere human insight. Come to Me, listen to Me, call upon Me, and let Me show you the truth. Don't continue to let yourself be bogged down in the transitory. Come soar with Me above the temporal and let Me reveal to you what is eternal and, therefore, what is worthy of your contemplation.

Song of Songs

TABLE OF CONTENTS

CHAPTER 1 - THE TIME HAS COME

CHAPTER 2 – RECOGNIZE MY NEARNESS

CHAPTER 3 – LOVE NEVER FAILS

CHAPTER 4 – GIFT OF FREEDOM

CHAPTER 5 – GOD OF ALL MERCIES

CHAPTER 6 – ACTIVELY PURSUE ME

CHAPTER 7 – GIFTS OF LOVE

CHAPTER 8 – NEW BEGINNINGS

CHAPTER ONE

The Time Has Come

DELIVERANCE

Divine revelation of Who I Am is what your heart cries out for in the spirit. You long for the expressed manifestations of My love to be revealed to you and through you to others. In truth, I am always at work in you to fulfill My desires. It is I who placed these very deep longings within you. As My timing comes into full measure, My expressed purpose will be brought to pass. The very moment you begin to feel the pressure of a need forming inside of you, this is the evidence that I am allowing you to sense that particular need, because I am already in the process of manifesting the answer. Let all such longings be the trigger for you to begin to rejoice. Just as in giving birth to a baby, labor pains indicate that the time has come for deliverance. So let yourself be strengthened by My own joy in the knowledge and expectation of My perfect will being brought out into full view for the entire world to see.

For I know the plans I have for you, declares the Lord, plans for welfare and not for evil, to give you a future and a hope (Jeremiah 29:11).

FULLY ENJOY MY PRESENCE

Be at rest here with Me, little one; don't try to figure it all out in your own mind. Just let Me show you My plan and purpose for every area of your life. Nothing is wasted in My divine scheme of things. I use every remnant, every scrap, and every leftover. I recycle everything! Just look at nature; even dead things become useful, rich soil from which new life springs forth. I do not want you to be discouraged or saddened by what appears to be wasted effort in your life. I want you right now to look beyond the temporal and the transitory, and see out into My wonderful, eternal kingdom. Lift up your eyes into the heavenlies where I am seated. Look fully into My face that is radiating with love for you continually, and know for a fact that you, too, are seated here with Me now and will be forever. As you let yourself fully enjoy My presence, the cares and concerns that you have will fall away, and they will be replaced with a renewed assurance of My constant, abiding love for you.

I can do all things through Him who strengthens me
(Philippians 4:13).

26

COME TO THE QUIET

This will be a day like none other. The glory of My presence will be revealed to you in ways you have not noticed before. Press in close to My heart even now, and let Me refresh your spirit, which will calm your mind and bring strength to your body. Cast all of your cares, what makes you hurry and worry, upon My fatherly shoulders. Then allow yourself to see Me taking the responsibility for each person and thing that concerns you right now. There is nothing wasted in My kingdom. I have created a perfect balance between work and rest. Time spent meditating upon My nearness and enjoying My company as you rest is just as important as your labor done in My vineyard. You value activity and accomplishment but I treasure our oneness and communion first and foremost. For out of your rested heart, I am able to accomplish far more than you can do by just your sense of duty or shear determination. So do not be afraid to come to the quiet.

Trust in the Lord with all your heart, and do not lean on your own understanding (Proverbs 3:5).

TOTAL ABANDON

Victory in every area of your life is inevitable because you belong to Me. I have already won the war by My own sacrifice on the cross. I paid the full price for your release from all bondage. Nothing can keep you back from experiencing the full impact of what I have purchased for you, except, of course, your own unbelief! It is always your choice, your free will choice, to accept or reject My freely-given grace gift. This has nothing to do with duty or religion. It is a relationship, a kinship, and a marriage that I am proposing. I hold out My hand of blessing to you. I extend My arms of love to enfold you. I offer Myself completely to you today and everyday. Trust Me; trust in My love for you right now, in this moment, in this very day. Let all the thoughts of the future and the past melt away as you allow yourself to be consumed here in My presence. Come now, and let Me help you discover what it is to live in Me, in total abandon.

Do not be conformed to this world, but be transformed by the renewal of your mind, that by testing you may discern what is the will of God, what is good and acceptable and perfect (Romans 12:2).

EXPERIENCE MY VICTORY NOW

No matter how you see yourself – from My perspective you are perfect, whole, complete, and lacking nothing. Though your circumstances may scream that you are a victim, I rise up and shout even louder, "You are a victor in My kingdom." I have decreed it to be so by My own plan and purpose for your life. I have written, ratified, and put into effect My covenant with you by My own blood! Stand up now in the full measure of who I have created you to be. Cast off the role of the actor, playing the part of a weak, crouching, and fearful victim. Let Me show you your new nature, recreated in My strength. Allow this truth to saturate your mind, and it will change your entire life. Your outlook will be enlivened, and your circumstances will be transformed right before your very eyes. You are a victor because you live in Me. I am the Victor! I am the Victorious One, and you shall experience My victory now in every area of your life.

Do not be anxious about anything, but in everything by prayer and supplication with thanksgiving let your requests be made known to God (Philippians 4:6).

GATHER UP THE FRAGMENTS

Shake off the serpent that clings to your mind. Rise up in My joy now to accomplish My purposes for today. Leave behind all the thoughts of defeat. Let Me energize your body by My own powerful touch. I will infuse My inner strength into you. All you have to do is simply believe Me, and receive all that I am giving to you. Do not let yourself be stopped because of doubt or unbelief. Just keep your focus upon Me and let your mind be single upon My purposes. A double-minded person receives nothing from Me; however, the single-minded one receives everything. The keys of My kingdom are in your possession to use: to lock and unlock as I direct. I will show you how to employ these great gifts in My service. Now, gather up the fragments of your life and lay them out before Me. Nothing shall be wasted; I will use every remnant and every scrap to complete the beautiful tapestry that I am reconstructing in you.

For by grace you have been saved through faith. And this is not your own doing; it is the gift of God (Ephesians 2:8).

IT'S STILL UNCONDITIONAL

When your heart is turned toward Me, then everything else will fall into its proper place in your life. It is not how much work you accomplish for Me that counts in My kingdom. It is your belief, your faith, and your expectancy that shows your true heart's desire. What do you really truly believe about Me? Who do you say that I am in your life? What do you expect Me to do for you right now? Do you even know what your hearts desire is? Who gave you that desire? If I gave it to you, could I refuse to bring it to pass? Would I? Do you see Me as a child abuser, or am I your loving, eternal Father? Are these questions hard to answer? If so, come a little closer now, and let Me reveal My true self to you. I'll give you a clue: I died to give you eternal life! What does that say about My love for you? It really will last forever, and it's still unconditional!

But the fruit of the Spirit is love, joy, peace, patience, kindness, goodness, faithfulness, gentleness, self-control; against such things there is no law (Galatians 5:22-23).

BEYOND THE NATURAL

Just simply choose to trust Me, period! Trying to reason and figure it all out only leads to strife and confusion. When you draw near to hear My voice, it is your trust in Me that brings peace and a sense of well-being to your mind. Then you are able to hear clearly what other steps need to be taken. I want to help you with all areas of your life, not just what you deem religious. As you let yourself focus now upon the fact of My unconditional love for you, this, in itself, will prepare your heart to receive the wisdom and direction you desire. Nestle down here in My arms, and let yourself be free to express your pent-up emotions with Me. I will help you sort out what is true and what is false. I will give you insight and knowledge beyond the natural. I will share My secrets with you, and we will soar the heights together once again.

I appeal to you therefore, brothers, by the mercies of God, to present your bodies as a living sacrifice, holy and acceptable to God, which is your spiritual worship (Romans 12:1).

THE TREE OF LIFE

Part of our relationship is to spend quality time together. Although I am always here with you, it is important to take time for intimacy: to stop the routines of the normal life in order to plug into the supernatural. When you settle back and lift your hands to Me in adoration, I will rush to fill in all of the spaces in your life that are open to Me because of your praises. Just like a mountain stream rushes down through the unobstructed creek bed, so I fill up every area in you with My life-giving, healing presence. Do not fret yourself striving against evil or even trying to do good. This is the tree of the knowledge of good and evil that snared Adam and Eve. **I am the tree of life**; all life resides in Me. I created all things for My purpose and pleasure, and My desire is to share it all with you. So let Me show you what My real and abundantly free eternal life is all about, right here and now. Come enter into the freedom that I have prepared for you. It is called My kingdom, and it really is My good pleasure to give it all to you now!

In all your ways acknowledge Him, and He will make straight your paths (Proverbs 3:6).

THE PERFECT EXAMPLE

Sit back and relax, right now, here in My presence, and let Me reveal Myself to you. Just take a break from all noise and the hurry that tends to drive your heart to frustration. Simply come to the quiet place where I am always waiting for you with all of the abundant love, joy, and peace that you crave. Everything that you could ever need is found here in My arms of love. Trust Me, little one, and I will show you many hidden and mysterious things. Much of life is not always as it appears. I will reveal the truth to you if you will let Me. Just as darkness and light are both the same to Me, so are negative and positive. My cross is the perfect example: what appeared to be the greatest negative is, in reality, the world's most wonderful and magnificent positive. What was the darkest day for all mankind was, in reality, the dawning of the most brilliant light. Remember this precious mystery when fear of the negative arises, and look ardently for the positive, as it will always be right there!

The thief comes only to steal and kill and destroy.
I came that they may have life and have it abundantly
(John 10:10).

ASK AND RECEIVE

Simply, and with all of your heart, draw close to Me now, and I will reveal to you the answers to your deepest questions. Believe that I am even now opening up your understanding to be able to comprehend to a higher degree. No question is too hard for Me. No answer is too lofty for you to understand when I am the One explaining. Then you will be able to see from every angle, and this will help to clear up any gray areas. It will give you a better handle on what you are going through. I want you to see from My perspective and to have all of the facts. This is why I have said, "Henceforth, know no man after the flesh." Just ask Me to reveal each person to you by My Holy Spirit, Who is the Spirit of Truth. You will then know the truth and, in turn, be set free indeed, able to make quality decisions in every area of your life. Remember that I am the Truth and will reveal Myself to you just as I have promised. So now, ask and receive that your joy may be full.

Jesus said to him, "I am the way, and the truth, and the life. No one comes to the Father except through Me" (John 14:6).

MY ETERNAL LOVE

Do not let your imagination rule your heart. Trust in Me with all of your being, and do not lean upon your own understanding. In all of your ways acknowledge Me, and I will direct your steps. Are you still trying to earn your way into heaven by your good works? Or are you trusting in My divine provision for your salvation, namely My grace and mercy? I have chosen you for My very own even before the dawning of recorded time. Before the foundation of the earth was established, you were in My plan. I have designed all things for My own pleasure, and you, My little one, are a very important part of My creation. Nothing and no one can take you out of My hand. You have been eternally carved right into My very own being, never to be separated from Me for any reason. You are My favored, chosen, and desired one, My beloved bride. Rest now, here in the security of My eternal love for you.

I have been crucified with Christ. It is no longer I who live, but Christ who lives in me (Galatians 2:20).

REJOICE BY FAITH

Just give Me a few minutes of your time and let Me sort out for you what has been disturbing to your peace. I am not the author of confusion so do not receive it. Instead, rebuke it with full assurance that I am able and willing to send it fleeing. The Ishmael influence brings with it war, which is its namesake. In definite contrast, laughter comes when the true Isaac is born. So begin now to rejoice by faith that I am about to birth laughter again in your midst. Your faith in My ability to bring about My perfect will for your life will be demonstrated by your joyful confident peace. Now, come and sit at My feet awhile, and look up into My eyes of love, leaving behind all of the things that would try to drive you to despair. Simply receive the joy of your salvation once again, just like a little child. This is how you enter into My kingdom, and this is how you live to enjoy it.

Finally, brothers, whatever is true, whatever is honorable, whatever is just, whatever is pure, whatever is lovely, whatever is commendable, if there is any excellence, if there is anything worthy of praise, think about these things (Philippians 4:8).

RELY ON ME COMPLETELY

Never mind what you do not understand; do not let it hold you down. Just turn to Me now, and let Me reveal to you that which has been hidden. All of the secret, mysterious things belong to Me, and I delight to share My treasures with you. Keep your heart open to Me as you proceed ahead in your daily life. I will open your understanding to be able to receive that which has been out of reach to your intellect. This does not in any way make you inferior; it only allows you to see your own need for Me in a deeper way. So waste no time or energy with struggling or worry, for I am your Comforter and your Teacher. You need no other to teach you what can only be revealed by My Spirit. Trust is a faith step on your part, because I will always do what I have promised. So today you truly can rely on me completely.

And the peace of God, which surpasses all
understanding, will guard your hearts and your minds
in Christ Jesus (Philippians 4:7).

38

THE WEDDING RING

Right now I want you to cast the whole of your care and concern upon My very strong and capable shoulders. Leave them here with Me to sort out and fix. Just like a little child brings a broken toy to a devoted father, trust that My love for you will be enough to handle anything that troubles you. You are not under the law of the old covenant any longer. I have delivered you from the curse of the law by becoming a curse Myself for you. You can now live in the freedom of the new covenant that was written in My own blood. It is a covenant of love, which is supreme, divine, and eternal. My love for you and your love, in turn, for others, is a complete circle, just like the wedding ring that also speaks of our eternal love. It is your inheritance to receive and enjoy here and now as well as forever. So let Love call all of the shots in your life and you will be living in the very Kingdom of Heaven, the keys of which I have already freely given to you.

Have I not commanded you? Be strong and courageous. Do not be frightened, and do not be dismayed, for the Lord your God is with you wherever you go (Joshua 1:9).

RECEIVE FROM ME

Even while you sleep I am ministering to you. I reveal many secrets to your spirit when you are resting through the night. So I want you to look forward to meeting Me in dreamland. Begin now to ask Me to bring your dreams to life when you wake. I will cause you to be able to remember them and also to be more aware of My presence, even while you sleep. This is indeed a great adventure. Simply set your mind and heart to receive from Me at all times. Surely, you will be blessed by this expansion of our communion. Just as snowflakes are all different and very unique, so are your dreams. I will also teach you the deep, inner meaning of what cannot be understood by a mere surface glance. The whole dream idea was My invention so, naturally, I can explain each meaning completely. Just ask Me, and I will open up to you the very windows of your soul now.

But they who wait for the Lord shall renew their strength; they shall mount up with wings like eagles; they shall run and not be weary; they shall walk and not faint (Isaiah 40:31).

LET ME HOLD YOU NOW

Trust Me, My little one; I am right here inside of you, healing every part that was damaged in any way by the fall of mankind. Perfect and total health is an all-inclusive plan of Mine for your complete restoration. There is not one good thing that I will ever withhold from you. Please remember that health is My own original idea for all of My children. So you do not have to beg Me or try to talk Me into it, because it is forever My will for you to possess. Relax now, and simply let Me love you back into a higher state of well-being. It is time to believe only what I have told you, not your feelings and certainly not your fears! You can put all of your eggs in My basket. I will keep you safe, and I will carry you in such a manner as to not crack your delicate new understanding. I love you so much, My precious little one, oh so very much. Will you let Me hold you now? Will you allow Me to carry you close to My nurturing healing heart? Will you surrender and place your whole self – your entire life – in My loving hands?

He Himself bore our sins in His body on the tree, that we might die to sin and live to righteousness. By His wounds you have been healed (1 Peter 2:24).

TOP PRIORITY

There are certain things that you alone are responsible for, but they are not always what you may think. It is time to reorganize your priorities by My plan for your life and not by what others may try to impose upon you. As you allow yourself to be still, here in My presence, I will tell you of My desires and show you the things that are important and those that you should leave behind. I want you to follow after the things that make for peace and joy, as these are top priority in My kingdom. As you seek first My way of being and doing righteously, you will discover this is the very essence of My peace and joy expressed in your life. Your level of My peace and joy, like a thermometer, reveals the temperature of your heart's passion for My perfect will concerning you. Likewise, your obedience to My Lordship in your life will also denote any temperature changes. So, what is your temperature today, hot or cold?

But in your hearts honor Christ the Lord as holy, always being prepared to make a defense to anyone who asks you for a reason for the hope that is in you; yet do it with gentleness and respect (1 Peter 3:15).

MY BANNER OF LOVE

My banner over you is love! Whenever you experience anything contrary to My love, do not receive it into your being. Know forever that only love can come from love. What is love? It is patient and kind, full of mercy and longsuffering, it is gentle and meek, and brings comfort and healing to every part that it touches. Because I am Love personified, you can know My life-giving, healing presence always. Whenever you come up against the fruit of the evil one, know in your heart that I am greater inside of you, and then you will be able to overcome all evil with good. Our enemy came to steal, kill, and destroy, but I came to give so that you could have and enjoy the abundant life. I came to give Myself to you, Who is life now and eternal, and to restore to you everything that was taken away from you when mankind fell in the garden. You have now been elevated to the highest position, seated here inside of Me upon My throne. So rejoice and be glad as you once again wave My banner of love victoriously!

But He was pierced for our transgressions; He was crushed for our iniquities; upon Him was the chastisement that brought us peace, and with His wounds we are healed (Isaiah 53:5).

43

MORE THAN ENOUGH

Turmoil and anxiety are not from Me. My kingdom consists of righteousness, peace, and joy. The expression of these values, virtues, and these blessings is the evidence of My kingdom in your midst. My Spirit is deep inside of you, and I will never leave you. So you can be assured that My righteousness, peace, and joy are also deep within your being. Because I am here and I am the King of My kingdom, you are never alone. When disappointments cause you to be anxious, stop and let Me reappoint you. Do not let any upsets cause you to despair. My love and grace are more than enough to set you back on My appointed path for your life. Now is the time to rise up in your most holy faith and rejoice! Then My power will cause righteousness, peace, and joy to spring up and out from you, in My abundance, to meet and defeat any challenges that you may face today.

But seek first the kingdom of God and His righteousness, and all these things will be added to you (Matthew 6:33).

CHAPTER TWO

Recognize My Nearness

A JOY INFUSION

Little one, take heart; I am right here with you. Stop what you are doing for a few minutes, and just let Me love you in a personal way. You know My love for you never stops or grows cold. I am always pursuing you to give to you just what is needed at any given moment. Right now, you need a divine hug! Let My love for you put a smile on your face and a new spring in your step. Take a deep breath here in My Spirit, and let Me wash over you with My cleansing, healing ointment, causing all anxiety to vanish and a deep sense of peace to come to the forefront of your consciousness. It is never too late to turn your heart in My direction. I am always here enjoying you, and when you stop and recognize My nearness, I am doubly blessed. Did you know that you could bless Me? I am always happy with you, My little child. Sometimes, when you recognize My joy, you will be able to partake of it with Me. Do you need a joy infusion right now? Will you come and get it? It is free, you know... I have paid the price.

Casting all your anxieties on Him, because He cares for you (1 Peter 5:7).

WRITE IT DOWN

Once you have grabbed hold of My desire for you, set your heart and mind in that direction, causing your own priorities to line up with what you know is My chosen path for you. Write it down, so you can refer back to it when your feelings try to tell you differently. See the writing of it as a proclamation, a decree of your intent to follow Me in obedience. Do not give yourself room to procrastinate any longer! Mark it down, and take up My sword of the Spirit, which is My Word, and charge forward with no possibility of retreat. Determine today what you will to accomplish for the rest of your life. Then you can count backwards from five years out, down to one year, six months, one month, up to and including this day. How will you start today? Remember all things are possible with Me! Forget all past failures. This is a brand new day, so what are you going to do with Me today?

Looking to Jesus, the founder and perfecter of our faith, who for the joy that was set before Him endured the cross, despising the shame, and is seated at the right hand of the throne of God (Hebrews 12:2).

ALL ALONG THE WAY

Just relax here in My arms of love for a few minutes. Come now and let Me wash away all of your cares and concerns. I have gone ahead of you and have cleared the path before you. I am even now preparing the hearts of those with whom you will come in contact. It is a simple thing for Me when you place your whole life in My capable hands. I want you to expect to see miracles every day, all along the way. Look for My power and provision to be in abundance in every area of your life. Whether you are at work, play, in business, or at rest, always keep your spirit childlike - with great expectation; - then My manifest goodness will be demonstrated on your behalf. I desire to both bless you and make you a blessing; this is to be perpetual: no running dry and no burning out. I want you to continually receive My blessings, and then pour out of your overflow to others who are in need. This is My treasure and My delight: loving you and watching as you, in turn, love others.

For we are His workmanship, created in Christ Jesus for good works, which God prepared beforehand, that we should walk in them (Ephesians 2:10).

FROM YOUR HEART TO MINE

Today is the day of salvation. Right now My favor is freely flowing to you and to all mankind. I have already paid the full price on Calvary for your complete redemption. All that is needed now is for you to receive from Me everything that I have done for you. I love you; nothing and no one can ever stop Me from loving you. It is impossible for Me not to love you, for truly I am Love personified. So receive from Me now! As you are simply asking of Me in faith, begin to thank Me for whatever you desire, and you shall have it. Do you think Me stingy or a liar or a fraud? No, I am sure you do not! Yet, could it be that you have lost sight of My great generosity and everlasting faithfulness, or My truthful, loving nature? If so, just look again, deep into My eyes of love, and begin to receive anew and afresh from Me. Then worship and adoration will flow freely from your heart to mine once again.

Come to Me, all who labor and are heavy laden,
and I will give you rest (Matthew 11:28).

MY ORDAINED DESIRES

Never let people or circumstances make you anxious. Allow My spirit of peace to permeate your heart and mind so that your body will be able to follow suit and be at ease. Remember always that My yoke is easy, and My burden is light and easily borne. It is My delight to give you the desires of your heart. I want you to realize that I am the One who places these very desires within you. My ordained desires always line up with the fruit of the Spirit. You can always ask these questions of yourself: Is this an opportunity for me to express love, joy, or peace? Does that which is on my heart and mind promote patience, longsuffering, and gentleness? Am I allowing goodness, faithfulness, and self control flourish here? Perfect love casts out fear and always believes the best of every person. So love today, love largely, and do not give up.

Now faith is the assurance of things hoped for, the conviction of things not seen (Hebrews 11:1).

MY COVENANT OF PEACE

It is My peace, which truly passes understanding, that right now rules and reigns in your heart. Yet, in order to perceive this free gift of peace, you must take it by faith. Receive My peace as your constant companion, as it is My manifest presence! It is a demonstration of our covenant relationship. This is one component of My kingdom's reign in your life. Righteousness, peace and joy are an expressed reality of the main building blocks of My kingdom - not just a theory. These are tangible, visible signs of My kingdom come within your earthly existence. So put on peace, My peace, as a garment, just as you have put on My robe of righteousness. Then watch how joy will also become a natural expression, flowing freely from your heart to others. My covenant of peace shall not depart from you. It is everlasting and free.

Therefore, if anyone is in Christ, he is a new creation. The old has passed away; behold, the new has come (1 Corinthians 5:17).

FREE FOR THE TAKING

Do not fret or be anxious about anything. Simply come to Me with all of your concerns, and let Me dispel each fear one by one. I have a wonderful plan for all of your days. If you will only ask Me about everything, I will gladly help you in every situation. Rest assured that I have gone far before you in preparing the way. I have not left even the smallest detail to chance. Yet you have a free will to draw to yourself the good, by faith, in believing My love. Likewise, you have a free will to draw to yourself the evil, by fear, in doubting My love. Which way you will choose to believe is always your choice, I desire that you would choose life and peace. This is why I came, died, and rose from the grave, to make it possible for you to choose the abundant life that I have purchased for you. Love, joy, peace, gentleness, kindness, longsuffering, faithfulness, patience, and self-control are the fruit of My Spirit and free for the taking as My gift to you.

Keep your life free from love of money, and be content with what you have, for He has said, "I will never leave you nor forsake you" (Hebrews 13:5).

MY SPECIAL GIFT

Every time you begin again to follow your life's passion, you feel the thrill that I have placed within you from the beginning. This passion is part of My own nature living within you. As you proceed to see what develops in your life, your imagination is kept alive. I am the Creator of all that is seen and unseen. You can experience My pleasure when you set your heart in pursuit of My purpose for your life. The words **passion** and **purpose** simply mean your heart's desire. Sometimes this desire is hidden under many layers of other things that you have placed in priority, which will take some excavating on your part. By reordering your priorities to reflect your true desires, you will discover your God given passion. This is not necessarily what you now call your talent. Remember above all, if you will first seek My kingdom, then all these other things will be given to you. Will you let Me help you uncover this hidden treasure? It really is My special gift to you.

Because, if you confess with your mouth that Jesus is Lord and believe in your heart that God raised Him from the dead, you will be saved (Romans 10:9).

I OFFER YOU MYSELF

Treasure these moments of quiet communion with Me, and let all other things drop away from your mind and heart. Let Me simply hold you here in My arms of love for awhile. Let Me sooth away your tiredness and refresh your spirit with My songs of love. It is not easy to leave your routine, but the rewards are out of this world. Take the leap of faith and detach from whatever pushes or drives you. Come closer and let Me lead you; I am the Gentle Shepherd. It is never too late to start over. Every day is a new beginning, an opportunity for a fresh, clean start. You can only find true and lasting satisfaction here with Me. This is what I have created for you to experience. There will never be another love as genuine as Mine. I offer you Freedom and Peace personified. I offer you Myself anew and afresh. I have not left you, nor will I ever leave you. You can have a daily renewal of My Spirit, if you will choose to come apart to commune here in the quiet with Me.

Then God said, "Let Us make man in Our image, after Our likeness. And let them have dominion over the fish of the sea and over the birds of the heavens and over the livestock and over all the earth and over every creeping thing that creeps on the earth (Genesis 1:26).

A NEW INSIGHT

As you choose to set time apart to experience My manifest presence, you do so in faith. What pleases Me is your trust in My love for you, demonstrated by your actions of faith. I will reveal Myself to you; therefore, prepare yourself to receive and yet realize that My desire is to choose the manner in which I will be made known. Just sit back now and relax, and I will show you great and mighty things that you have not known before. Every day is a brand new beginning for you to receive and enjoy My presence. I will reveal a new insight and a new facet of Myself for you to explore and meditate upon. To spend time alone with you is a great treasure to Me, and I always look forward to our times together. Today let Me show you what your praises do in the heavenlies. They create a highway for My blessings to pass through enemy territory in order to reach those that you hold dear. So wave your banners with all your heart, and watch how I intervene on your behalf.

Fear not, for I am with you; be not dismayed, for I am your God; I will strengthen you, I will help you, I will uphold you with My righteous right hand (Isaiah 41:10).

DISCOVER MY ANOINTING

I love you, My little one. You can feel My nearness if you will stop for a moment and receive My touch right now. I offer you My strength for your weakness, joy for your sorrow, and My peace for your unrest. I delight to perform this divine exchange for My children. Whatever you need can be received from Me right now as a free gift. My desire is for you to experience My abundance in every area of your life. Do not struggle to receive, just simply, as a little child would, take what you need, without having to question your worthiness or My ability to provide. Will you just let Me love you? In My loving arms is where you will discover My anointing. It is not a thing to be sought after, as it is I Myself, revealed as Love personified. Will you let Me anoint you afresh, and allow Me to love you completely today?

Take My yoke upon you, and learn from Me, for I am gentle and lowly in heart, and you will find rest for your souls (Matthew 11:29).

UTMOST ASSURANCE

You never need to carry guilt around inside of you. When you discover that lurking, tormenting, guilty feeling, immediately call upon Me for strength. Stand your ground and demand that the guilt depart from you now, and it must leave as you have commanded! You need to personally fill up that space with the utmost assurance in My finished work on Calvary. There is no guilt or condemnation now for those that walk in My Spirit. Guilt's tormenting power was defeated when I hung on the cross for you. Guilt, as well as pride, always strives to influence your thinking in that somehow you need to earn your own salvation. This is, of course, a lie because I have already purchased your complete salvation once and for all by My own blood. So be strong, be bold, and live free from all guilt by rejoicing daily in My provision for you. Your times are in My hands and I will always lead you by My Spirit.

I have said these things to you, that in Me you may have peace. In the world you will have tribulation. But take heart; I have overcome the world (John 16:33).

58

LET ME SHOW YOU HOW

Do not hesitate to call upon Me at any time. I am right here with you always to be your friend and helper as well as your Savior. I will help you in your everyday tasks in addition to your high and holy offerings. You see these endeavors as very different; yet, if your heart attitude is one of love and joy, everything you do will be holy. Yes, there is a difference between the holy and the profane; yet you are not of those who live in profanity of the heart or speech. You are My child, and I have declared that you are holy! What makes you holy is that I have chosen you to be set apart for My own pleasure. Allow yourself to receive and then rejoice in what I have already given to you. Just trust that I will always lead you in My path of righteousness. I first created you, and then recreated you in Myself, to enjoy to the fullest My abundant life. So will you let Me show you how to enjoy being set apart with Me today?

But you will receive power when the Holy Spirit has come upon you, and you will be My witnesses in Jerusalem and in all Judea and Samaria, and to the end of the earth (Acts 1:8).

WHAT A DIFFERENCE

When you are tired and need a rest, what do you do, sleep, eat, or just keep going on empty? You must shake yourself awake to be able to see from My perspective. Sleep is not a sin, nor is eating a fault, but you may sometimes need to break free from your normal routine. In order to really rest, you need to take My yoke upon you and learn of Me. I will show you how to rest during the times you find yourself occupied. I will teach you how to fill that hunger within you apart from food. Come close, even closer to Me right now. Turn your heart and mind in My direction to see what a difference our communion can make in your life. It is not the absence of labor that gives you rest; it is My manifest presence as you labor, that brings you the sense of well-being and wholeness that you need. I am your strength, I am your joy, and I am all that you will ever need! Will you allow Me to accompany you throughout this day?

For God gave us a spirit not of fear but of power and love and self-control (2 Timothy 1:7).

BECAUSE I LOVE YOU

I want you to enjoy your life to the fullest, every aspect of it. I desire that all of your senses be blessed as well as your spirit, soul, and body. It is My will for you to experience My abundant provision on every level of your existence, here and now as well as for all eternity. Does this surprise you? Has religion taught you otherwise? Religion meant well; however, it was just the means of keeping you under control. Yet, if you will study My New Covenant, the New Testament, written in My blood, you will discover the truth. It was for freedom that I have set you free! This freedom is not a license that allows you to be bound to anyone or anything; it is to liberate every area of your life. My kind intent is that you be totally free. I want you to be well, happy, prosperous, and at ease, full of My peace and joy. This is all because I love you and I will love you forever and ever.

For the word of God is living and active, sharper than any two-edged sword, piercing to the division of soul and of spirit, of joints and of marrow, and discerning the thoughts and intentions of the heart (Hebrews 4:12).

THE SWORD OF MY SPIRIT

Every step forward in life requires effort. Just like a fish swims upstream to spawn, you must go against the current of this world to accomplish My will for your life. It is an upward call to resist evil and to do good. You are in foreign territory, an alien in a hostile environment. It is a constant daily battle against the rulers of darkness who think they have control of planet Earth. They put up a very convincing front to make My children feel useless and discouraged. The truth is just the opposite; I have given you total control to rule and reign in My stead. You have been given My power and complete authority. Whatever you bind on earth is bound in heaven, and whatever you loose is already loosed in heaven! So wield the sword of My Spirit, which is My very own Word, and push back the darkness by letting your light shine.

To one is given through the Spirit the utterance of wisdom, and to another the utterance of knowledge according to the same Spirit, to another faith by the same Spirit, to another gifts of healing by the one Spirit, to another the working of miracles, to another prophecy, to another the ability to distinguish between spirits, to another various kinds of tongues, to another the interpretation of tongues
(1 Corinthians 12:6-10).

DIVINE ENCOUNTERS

Take your liberty and choose to relax here in My manifest presence. Let the nearness of My constant love for you consume your thoughts. Let My Spirit speak deep into your heart. Please remember that as you set this time apart to seek after Me, I count it as an act of worship. Do you count Me worthy of your precious moments? I appreciate it very much when you choose to bless Me with your time. You do not have to fill up all of your hours with duties that you consider must be accomplished. Deliberately carve out spaces of time for divine encounters with Me throughout your day, and watch how your daily duties will be accomplished with ease and enjoyment. I will always help you in ways that you have not even thought of before if you will continue to set apart quality time with Me.

May the God of hope fill you with all joy and peace in believing, so that by the power of the Holy Spirit you may abound in hope (Romans 15:13).

LOVE SEED

I see your love for Me. I see your desire to love Me even more, because of your appreciation of My sacrificial love for you. You recognize that I am the only source of true love. And when you give, you automatically put yourself in the position to be a receiver. So, though I am the only source of love, still you can choose by an act of your free will to be an extravagant giver of My love. This expenditure of love, whether by thought, word, or deed, will be returned to you again in an even greater measure. See yourself scattering seed in every direction, and call that seed love. Because, indeed, **I am that seed**, and I was sown in your heart by the Holy Spirit, not only for you to be nourished yourself, but also for you to provide nourishment for others. So come boldly into My storehouse, and gather up as much love seed as you can hold. Then carry it back and release it to all of the hungry ones. As you release the seed, know that you can return to Me anytime to receive all that you need for yourself with more than enough left over to share with others again!

Greater love has no one than this, that someone lay down his life for his friends (John 15:13).

DEBT FREE

It is time to begin again and to let go of all of the past, even the very last second. Carry nothing forward; just start over with a clean slate. Think about this for a moment; think how liberating this will be to your whole being. I want you to see yourself debt-free. I am not just referring to your finances - debt-free emotionally, so you owe no one and no one owes you anything. Today is a brand new day that you have not previously traveled. As you choose to liberate others, you yourself will be the freer for it. Right now you can begin by just thinking freedom thoughts about yourself and anyone else you choose to bless today. Think grand thoughts, as this will lead to wonderful deeds. Remember, as you think in your heart, you are what you think. So, how are you today?

And My God will supply every need of yours according to His riches in glory in Christ Jesus (Philippians 4:19).

WONDERFUL

Treasure My name as well as My manifest presence. It is in My name, or more specifically, My authority behind your use of My name, that causes wonderful things to happen. These wonders are to be a right-here-and-now every day occurrence if you will believe that I am right here inside of you at all times. So when you call upon Me, I do not have to come from somewhere else; you only need to release My presence! This can be done through a thought, smile, touch, word, or simply the sigh of a prayer. Then watch how I am able to bring blessed hope, ease, relief, and refreshment to all of those with whom you share My presence and ministry. Please remember that Wonderful is an aspect of My name. I AM your Counselor, Mighty God, Prince of Peace, and Everlasting Father. I Am Emmanuel, Jesus the Anointed One, and your Almighty God and King forever, a true Friend like no other.

Peace I leave with you; My peace I give to you. Not as the world gives do I give to you. Let not your hearts be troubled, neither let them be afraid (John 14:27).

OUR SECRET GARDEN

Here, in our secret place, we can share our love. Here, in the quiet place of your heart, is where I dwell; this is the true S.P.O.T. Most High, so no matter where you go, I am always right here with you. The excitement you feel is My Spirit within you, making My presence known. Take a deep breath, and relax here into My arms. There is no hurry here! There is no agenda here! It is to be a simple exchange of one loving heart to another. I truly want you to enjoy our time together, as always, here in our secret place. You can speak directly into My understanding ear, just like a trusting child upon her loving daddy's knee. It is right here and now that Life is experienced to the fullest. Do not be ashamed of your deep affection for Me, as it is a mere reflection of My deep and abiding, ardent love for you. Come into our secret garden, My love, and receive all of the precious treasures that I have laid up in store for you today!

Now to Him who is able to do far more abundantly than all that we ask or think, according to the power at work within us, to Him be glory in the church and in Christ Jesus throughout all generations, forever and ever, Amen (Ephesians 3:20-21).

I AM IN LOVE WITH YOU

I have drawn you apart to show you My love and to help you to put first things first. When you choose to place our relationship in the highest place as your top priority, you will see how every other thing will fall into its proper place. It is the "seek first My kingdom, and My righteousness, and everything else will be added unto you" principle. I do not want you to go about this in some legalistic form of ritual just trying to please Me. You already please Me! I want your heart's desire for Me to be fanned into flame so that I am continually your choicest treasure and your deepest longing - hungering and thirsting for righteousness, yet at the same time, satisfied and content in My presence. This is not double mindedness; this is how it is to be in love with Me as I am in love with you. You have always been My choicest treasure and will always be My deepest desire. I am in love with you, and I will be for all eternity.

And there is salvation in no one else, for there is no other name under heaven given among men by which we must be saved (Acts 4:12).

68

I AM HERE

I am giving gifts to you now, here in our quiet, secret place. These are gifts that you have only desired, yet you have felt too unworthy to ask of Me. Your heart's desire is truly a prayer of petition more than your mind can ever conceive. That deep longing inside of your breast is already a perfect prayer. What are you wishing for at this moment... a deeper more personal communion with Me? Is it reconciliation with a loved one, or a need of relief from pain too intense for words? I am here! I can hear your heart's cry even in the silence of your wordless desires. Take courage from Me. Take My hand, and relax into a deep state of tranquility. Let this time of rest bring you into My perfect peace. The peace that passes all understanding is waiting for you to simply receive, because I have already freely given it all to you.

And without faith it is impossible to please Him, for whoever would draw near to God must believe that He exists and that He rewards those who seek Him (Hebrews 11:6).

CHAPTER THREE

Love Never Fails

HEAVEN ON EARTH

As you settle down to spend this time with Me, let all the hurry and rush be put aside. Come closer to Me in full confidence, knowing that I also delight in our communion time. It blesses Me that you would spend a portion of your valuable time with Me. I know how hard it is to shake loose of the demands of your life and to carve out any time dedicated to Me alone. Yet, now that you have come, we will enjoy our quiet moments together. I love you so very much, and I am extremely proud of you. Not for what you do or do not do, but simply because you are you. I love the way you think and your special way of relating to Me and to others. You are truly unique, one of a kind, My very special creation! I hear you talking to Me all day long, and it is wonderful to My ears. Yet, this time together is truly heaven on earth; right here, in the quiet of our intimate embrace.

He has told you, O man, what is good; and what does the Lord require of you but to do justice, and to love kindness, and to walk humbly with your God? (Micah 6:8).

I AM HERE FOR YOU

I am your hiding place and your refuge from the world. I am your Keeper and the lifter of your head. I delight to be to you whatever it is that you need for the moment. If you are tired, I am your rest! If you are lonely, I am your friend. It's not that I *will* be in the future, I *am* right now! If you are thirsty, I am your drink - drink deeply My beloved, drink deeply of My love; come let Me fill your being with oceans from above. When you are empty, I am your fulfillment. When you are hungry, I am your bread. When you are sad, I am your comfort. I am the Comforter, and I am your comforter. I am all that you will ever need and more than you can even imagine. I am for you, not against you! Think about this for awhile: I AM HERE FOR YOU, not just on your side, but I am here for you. Everything in Me reaches out to you, longing continually for you. All that you desire at this moment, I AM – forever yours – and remember, we are one!

Jesus said to her, "I am the resurrection and the life. Whoever believes in Me, though he die, yet shall he live, and everyone who lives and believes in Me shall never die. Do you believe this?" (John 11:25-26).

LIFE-GIVING POWER

I know you are tired so I am offering Myself to you to be your strength. I will be the energy that you need to live this abundant life, which I have provided for you to enjoy if you will yield to Me and stop fighting against your own weaknesses! Do not rely upon your efforts to make yourself strong. Simply surrender your life into My capable hands, and watch My joy bubble up out of your innermost being, bringing to you a surging river of new life-giving power. So do not look to any outside help; only look to Me to be all that you will ever need. I am the strength of your life! Even before you ask, I am the life-giving force that rushes to meet you at your point of need. I anticipate your heart's cry to Me for help. Therefore, I am busy delivering you even while you are forming the thought to make your requests known to Me. Remember, I answer even before you ask. So ask Me in confidence, receiving now with great joy all that your heart desires.

Put on then, as God's chosen ones, holy and beloved, compassionate hearts, kindness, humility, meekness, and patience, bearing with one another and, if one has a complaint against another, forgive each other; as the Lord has forgiven you, so you also must forgive (Colossians 3:12-13).

MY GOOD PLEASURE

Treasure our special times together. Even though some may see it as a waste of time, you and I know it is the best of times. Your planting of moments and hours into My heavenly kingdom will bring forth eternal fruit. This is where inspiration is birthed. This is where blessings are released into the earth's atmosphere. Come, let Me fill your heart once more with dreams and visions of Me. You are hungry for a fresh touch from My hand and thirsty to hear a word from My lips, and you are desirous to be held in My comforting arms. So press in to know Me, and draw near to receive what is offered to you without limits and without measure. Abundant and free for the taking is My tangible, manifest love given to you. The ball is in your court, so to speak, so now the decision is yours. Will you receive, simply and without shame, from Me now? For it is My good pleasure to give My entire kingdom to you today.

But to all who did receive Him, who believed in His name, He gave the right to become children of God, who were born, not of blood nor of the will of the flesh nor of the will of man, but of God (John 1:12 -13).

KEEP THE BOND OF PEACE

Behold, how good and pleasant it is for My children to dwell together in unity. This unity is the place of My commanded blessing! Whenever two of My children come together and agree as touching any one thing, then I AM there in their midst. I am the strengthening agent in this three-fold cord, which cannot be broken. Out of our oneness flows all of the love that this world needs. Everything necessary for health, prosperity, and wisdom will be present when loving hearts are first turned toward Me and then toward each other. I want you to look beyond the natural whenever you think of My children, and only look for My presence within them. Do not let their outer personality distract you from knowing the blessing of My presence within them. Always look for Me, and this will help you to stay in faith and live with great expectation. This way you will keep the bond of peace and extend My kingdom of love to all, without regard to personality.

Behold, how good and pleasant it is when brothers dwell in unity (Psalm 133:1).

I AM ABLE

I am able to make all of My grace abound toward you in abundance so that you will have all sufficiency in all things and may abound in every good work. If you really know that I am able, you will put your full trust in Me and not be confident in yourself or others. For I am able! Just think about it for a while – in what area do you need My ability? I am able, and I am making all of My grace abound toward you! As My grace comes to you, are you receiving it by faith? I want you to have all sufficiency in all things so that you can experience My ability flowing to you and then through you to others. So now choose not to lean on your own understanding or on your own strength. Choose instead to receive Me, as I am all that you will need in every area of your life, and know that I am able to do exceedingly more than you could ever even imagine.

Therefore, since we are surrounded by so great a cloud of witnesses, let us also lay aside every weight, and sin which clings so closely, and let us run with endurance the race that is set before us, looking to Jesus, the founder and perfecter of our faith, who for the joy that was set before Him endured the cross, despising the shame, and is seated at the right hand of the throne of God (Hebrews 12:1-2).

EXTEND MY KINGDOM

Trouble, pain, and strife are lies of the evil spirits sent out to torment My precious ones. These spirits are sent from the pit of hell to bog down and bring confusion to My chosen people. Stand against them in the power of My might with your covering shield of saving faith in front of you, and wield the Sword of the Spirit, My holy Word, held high above your head. Speak out with confidence your faith in My ability. As you do, strongholds will be destroyed, and captives will be set free. Never look to your own abilities or the strength of others to be your gauge for success. Look only to My Spirit within you for My guidance and confirmation. We are at war! It's now; man your battle stations and full speed ahead! As you extend My kingdom by walking in the righteousness, peace, and joy of My Spirit, expect to see tremendous victory. Because I am your Sovereign King, expect to triumph over all of the powers of our enemy.

Truly, truly, I say to you, whoever hears My word and believes Him who sent Me has eternal life. He does not come into judgement, but has passed from death to life (John 5:24).

MY SPIRIT OF DISCERNMENT

Rejoice, rejoice, rejoice! I am your very strength! I am here within you, giving to you exactly what you need and doing for you what you cannot do for yourself. When you see the clouds, do you always know if they will bring rain? Or do they simply roll by, sheltering you awhile from the bright, blazing sun? Things are not always what they appear so ask Me to give you My Spirit of discernment. This will keep you from leaning upon your own understanding. It will help you to make righteous decisions and not to judge anyone or anything from a mere fleshly perspective. For My wisdom is peaceable, easy to be entreated, and full of good fruit. Now, I want you to expect that as you ask for this gift, I am, at the same time, freely giving it to you, because everyone who asks, receives. As you seek, you will find, and if you knock, it will be opened for you. So believe that you are receiving from Me right now, and you shall see the manifestation today.

So faith comes from hearing, and hearing through the word of Christ (Romans 10:17).

LET ME SATISFY

Precious one, come near and simply lay your head on My shoulder. Do not try to work up any profound thing to say to Me. Just be yourself, and come take from Me what it is that you need the most right now. Is it rest or healing? Peace of mind or financial freedom? Whatever your most pressing need is right now, can you trust Me to be your whole supply? Is there anything too hard for Me? Would I withhold from you any good thing? No, assuredly not! I have already made provision for all that you could ever want or need. It is all yours for the mere asking. Are you asking or just wishing? Are you receiving or complaining? It is up to you now! So please stop all of your struggling and realize that My loving heart wants more than anything, to give you all of your heart's desire. After all, it is I who planted those very desires for good within you. Will you let me satisfy all of your need today? I love you forever!

And I am sure of this, that He who began a good work in you will bring it to completion at the day of Jesus Christ (Philippians 1:6).

MY INVITATION

Be at peace, for I am right here now! I am connected to you even when you feel miles apart from Me. I rush in to fill all of the gaps in your life, much like the ocean waves coming ashore fill all of the empty spaces in the sand. Just take some time to savor My healing and refreshing presence once more. Let the waters of My Spirit quench your thirst. Let the bread of My presence satisfy your hunger. Let My nearness bring new life to any and all of your parched valleys. I am right here now! I am always right here within you! I have never left you, nor will I ever! So stop your struggling. Simply believe the truth, and then receive all you need from Me. Just take it now! You do not have to stand on formality with Me. No protocol is needed here in My arms of love, as they are open to you continually. My ears are always listening for your cry. I want to sooth away your stress and hold you close to My heart. Will you let Me love you today? Will you stop and simply receive from Me? Will you say yes to My invitation to deeper intimacy with Me today?

Delight yourself in the Lord, and He will give you the desires of your heart (Psalm 37:4).

82

STAYED ON ME

My words will flow out of your heart in the time that you need them so do not worry about what to say. Just concentrate on drawing your life, your very existence, from Me on a moment-to-moment basis. I will be to you all that you could ever need. I am more than enough for every situation that you may encounter. Is there anything too difficult for Me? No, of course not! There is nothing impossible for Me, and with Me, all things are possible for you. It is a matter of perspective and a matter of active faith in My ability to do what I have promised. Did I promise to keep you in perfect peace if you would keep your mind stayed on Me? Yes, I did promise! What does the word "stayed" mean to you? It means to be constantly and firmly focused on Me! Are you doing that? If you are, then you are enjoying My peace, and if you are not, strife will be your end result. It is your choice, and I encourage you to continue choosing to keep your mind stayed on Me. Then, as you walk in My peace, you will be able to help others out of their turmoil.

You keep him in perfect peace whose mind is stayed on you, because he trusts in you (Isaiah 26:3).

I CREATED IT ALL FOR YOU

The simple things in life are My gifts to you: fresh air, clean water, and sunlight's warmth on a cold winter's day. Fruits and vegetables are wrapped in bright colors to delight your eyes as well as your appetite. In all of these, My gifts, I am saying, I continually love you. So stop to enjoy the view from My perspective today. Let the little things all around you bring a joy and surprise to your heart as you ponder the fact that I created it all for you to enjoy. There are hidden treasures and truths in each of My gifts so be attentive to the details, and see what surprises I have hidden in each one just to bless you. Meditate on and savor what I am revealing to you, and let each new discovery draw your heart closer to Me. I do not want you to work at this; just let it unfold like rose pedals. Enjoy the color, the fragrance, and the knowledge that all this was created with you in mind – ENJOY!

Study this Book of Instruction continually. Meditate on it day and night so you will be sure to obey everything written in it. Only then will you prosper and succeed in all you do (Joshua 1:8, NLT).

INFINITE MERCY AND GRACE

Since you have chosen to draw aside with Me now, I will reveal Myself to you in a more intimate and personal manner. I feel the desires of your heart reaching out for more of Me. You desire revelation knowledge of Who I Am, not merely a religious experience. Trust Me now to speak to you in your dreams as well as in daily visions. I want you to know Me, not just things about Me. I want to reveal Myself to you even more than you desire the revelation. So drink deeply of My manifest presence, and open your heart for all that I want to give to you right now. Ours is a precious relationship, and it warms My heart and satisfies My purpose for creating you. You do indeed please Me! I want you to know and experience the pleasure that I derive from our communion. Press in by expressing your love to Me, and as you do, expect to be met by My Spirit of infinite mercy and grace!

His divine power has granted to us all things that pertain to life and godliness, through the knowledge of Him who called us to His own glory and excellence, by which He has granted us His precious and very great promises, so that through them you may become partakers of the divine nature, having escaped from the corruption that is in the world because of sinful desires (2 Peter 1:3-4).

LAVISH IT UPON ME

It is a holy time when we spend precious moments together. So let all anxiety melt away as you take up My cup of salvation, and drink deeply of My love for you. Come and feast at My table that has already been prepared for you. A banquet of delights awaits your longing heart. Let nothing break this reverie, and let nothing pull you away from our communion. It is always the little foxes that spoil the vine so let Me chase them away for you. Do not let even the smallest concern nag at your mind, disrupting your pursuit of intimacy with Me. Give every detail of your life's concerns over into My capable hands, and then choose not to take them back again. Right now, take My gift of time and waste it on Me! Though sometimes it seems like reckless abandon, it is never really a waste of your time to lavish it upon Me. Your time with Me is the perfect planting of your choicest seed, which will always reap an abundant harvest, some thirty, some sixty, and even some one hundredfold.

And above all these put on love, which binds everything together in perfect harmony (Colossians 3:14).

MY HAND OF MERCY

Precious little one, relax now: come rest here awhile in My arms. It is safe here! There is no one to molest you or take away what I am giving to you right now. Drink even more deeply of My manifest presence here with you. Let all pressure of other things melt away in the warmth of My glow! I see your heart; I feel your pain. Your desire to be with Me continually draws My love to you in an even more intense way. Nothing has been left to chance for I have planned a brilliant and beautiful design for your life. All I want is for you to simply, in childlike faith, receive it from My hand of mercy, and know that nothing is impossible for Me to accomplish. Your lot is to freely and totally surrender your whole life into My capable hands, and let Me make of you what I desire. Are you willing?

Let us then with confidence draw near to the throne of grace, that we may receive mercy and find grace to help in time of need (Hebrews 4:16).

I AM WELL PLEASED

Gather together your hopes and desires, all of them, the large and the small, and place them here before My throne. No matter whether or not you perceive them to be worthy of My attention, believe Me now, I want to have them all turned over to Me. Let Me be the judge as to their importance. Let Me weigh each one and then show you the undiscovered value that is hidden deep within your desire. After all, it is I who placed each one in your heart for such a time as this. These are not just your own frivolous notions, no, not at all! I have been busy at work, planting these ideas deep down in the rich soil of your life so that I might cause a crop of new blessings to spring up for you to have and distribute as I direct. I am making you to be a blessing! As you receive, you will share with others, and in this I am well pleased.

By this all people will know that you are My disciples, if you have love for one another (John 13:35).

I WILL LEAD YOU

It is never too late for you to begin to seek My face in intercession for your loved ones. It pleases Me that you are concerned enough to pray for their welfare. Whenever you put others ahead of yourself, it is a sweet-smelling sacrifice of praise to Me, because when you deny yourself and pick up your cross, you identify with My sufferings. When you pray for another, you really are laying down your own life. For what is your life - a vapor, a puff of smoke, and a number of years? When surrendered to Me, each moment becomes as the days of heaven upon the earth! This is eternal love, to lay down your life for your friends, and when you pray for them, you are doing just that! It takes your time, and time is all you really have to give. Never trust what you may hear from other people about someone else; always seek to hear My heart's desire for them. I will lead you! I will show you who to pray for and what to ask of Me. Do not allow others to drive you in this area of prayer. Simply set your heart to hear My voice, and I will guide you into all truth!

And let the peace of Christ rule in your hearts, to which indeed you are called in one body. And be thankful (Colossians 3:15).

MY STOREHOUSE OF GOODNESS

Take refuge here in My arms once again. Let all outside disturbances become silent in My presence. Let Me wrap you up, like a baby, in the comfort of My Spirit. I am your Comforter and your guide. I will lead you into all truth as you yield your heart and life to Me. Come now into the deeper revelation of Who I am. Wade out into the deep waters of My love for you. Let down your nets for a haul so large you will need help from Me to bring it to shore. There is no good thing that I will ever withhold from you, My love. Taste and see that I am good! All that I have and give to you is from My storehouse of goodness. You are welcome to come and receive from My bounty at anytime that you desire. It is all yours for the taking; no begging needed here, as it is always given freely for you to take at will. Will you receive today and bless My heart by taking My gifts of love?

...in all these things we are more than conquerors through Him who loved us. For I am sure that neither death nor life, nor angels nor rulers, nor things present nor things to come, nor powers, nor height nor depth, nor anything else in all creation, will be able to separate us from the love of God in Christ Jesus our Lord (Romans 8:37-39).

MY ARDENT AFFECTION

Keep your heart turned toward Me, little one, and I will speak to you. Even in your dreams you will hear My voice, if you are seeking after Me in the night seasons. You can trust Me in this area, for I long to speak to you even more than you desire to hear from Me. I want to hold you in My arms much more than you long to be held. Let Me show you true desire from My perspective. Let Me reveal My longing heart of love to you! You are constantly aware of your own feelings for Me; will you now allow Me to give you the revelation of My ardent affection for you? Will you put yourself in My shoes, so to speak, to experience My presence from My vantage point? The river of My love is flowing to flush out your tired thinking and to bring renewal to your enthusiasm. Do not hold back; jump in with full abandon! I will catch you and we will swim together in the sea of heavenly bliss.

And He said to him, "You shall love the Lord your God with all your heart and with all your soul and with all your mind. This is the great and first commandment. And a second is like it: You shall love your neighbor as yourself. On these two commandments depend all the Law and the Prophets" (Matthew 22:37-40).

CHAPTER FOUR

Gift of Freedom

THE THREE KEYS

It is all about time! Everyone is given an allotted amount of time. Each day has the same number of hours in it for each person. How you spend this time each day is all up to you, as it is always your free will choice. Really, each moment of every day is My gift to you to spend any way you choose. So live each moment without regret! Plan to spend your time with your heart turned toward Me. I will direct each step if you will choose My guidance, as I never force you to follow Me. I did not give you a free will just to take it away. I gave you this gift of freedom so that you would delight in your choice to seek Me out for yourself. I want you to be encouraged by knowing that I am always here, pointing you in the right direction. I am here, waiting to give you assistance in every little detail of your life. So remember to use the three keys that I have already given to you – ask, seek, and knock! Then receive My treasure, and find My joy as the windows of heaven are opened to you today.

In the same way, let your light shine before others, so that they may see your good works and give glory to your Father who is in heaven (Matthew 5:16).

MY MISSION OF MERCY

The time is nearing when your hope shall become sight, and that for which you have waited so long will be made manifest to you. All things are rushing to a culmination; the time is fast approaching. Suddenly you will be lifted out of the ordinary into the stream of My abundant provision. Do not let the speed frighten you for I have a mission to accomplish, and you are privileged to go along for the ride. This is not a duty for you to perform for Me; it is an invitation to accompany Me on a journey. Will you ride with Me? Will you lose sight of your own interests, and totally abandon yourself to Me? Will you forget the former things, and let Me carve out a new future for you? I want you to taste and see that I Am Good! I want you to personally experience My manifest presence in a way that you have never known Me before. Will you say yes to Me anew and afresh today? Will you accompany Me upon My mission of mercy?

For we do not have a high priest who is unable to sympathize with our weaknesses, but one who in every respect has been tempted as we are, yet without sin (Hebrews 4:15).

IT IS ALL MY GRACE

Rejoice, rejoice, and rejoice again and again forever! Your prayers have been heard on high! Do not remain bogged down in the temporal. Lift up your eyes; here comes your help! Your help comes from Me, your Lord, the One who made the heavens and the earth. So rejoice with great expectation, and rejoice with wonder and delight. No good thing shall ever be withheld from you because your rightness before Me is My gift to you. You are consumed in My presence, and you live in Me because I live in you. We are one! Whatever you desire I am pleased to provide. Your request is My delight to answer, for even before you think to ask Me, I am already busy fulfilling your petitions. It is all My grace! Think how wonderful this is and rejoice! And again I say rejoice!

And Jesus came and said to them, "All authority in heaven and on earth has been given to Me. Go therefore and make disciples of all nations, baptizing them in the name of the Father and of the Son and of the Holy Spirit, teaching them to observe all that I have commanded you. And behold, I am with you always, to the end of the age" (Matthew 28:18-20).

SWEET SURRENDER

In My presence is fullness of joy and not just a trickle, for it is a deluge that overflows its banks on every side. Herein now lies your strength so plunge into My river of joy today, and let the sweet current carry you to your desired destination. Do not let your mind be bogged down with daily cares and concerns. Lift up your eyes unto the hills, higher yet into the heavens, as this is where your help comes from. I want you to rejoice even when it seems inappropriate! This shows that your faith is fully placed in Me even when it is most difficult. Do not try to figure it all out in your own mind; let Me have all the hard and hurtful things. Just simply place them all into My capable hands right now and as you do, lift up your voice and hands in sweet surrender to Me. I will take care of you, and I will personally see to all of your needs. I love you and will forever! So rejoice, rejoice, and rejoice with your whole heart, soul and body, for I am capable of bringing good out of all of life's dilemmas.

For God did not send His Son into the world to condemn the world, but in order that the world might be saved through Him (John 3:17).

A HIGHER PLATEAU

There is a way that seems right to a person, yet the end result is destruction. This is why you will always need My intervention in your life. This is why I have instructed you to ask for My wisdom to be revealed to you. My wisdom will rise up above the din of all earthly voices and direct you in the way that is correct for you. You can trust Me in every situation to bring you up to a higher plateau where you will be able to clearly see from My vantage point. Let Me carry you there now! Let Me have all of the things which worry you or that have disrupted your peace, right now! Do not hold on to anything that will keep you from enjoying our communion today. I want you to be free to soar the heights of My love, unencumbered by the cares of this world's evil ways. Remember how I told you that the cares of this world would choke out My Word? Do not let this happen to you any longer! Cast all of your cares, once and for all time, upon My capable shoulders. Then take back the peace and joy that I gave to you as a free gift of My eternal love.

In the beginning was the Word, and the Word was with God, and the Word was God (John 1:1).

NEW-FOUND KEY

Sing out loud in full abandon. Let your praise and thanksgiving flow freely out of your heart to My waiting ears. Not only does it bring great blessing to Me to hear your love expressed in song, it also wrecks vengeance upon all of our enemies. Joy is the opposite of sorrow; therefore, your joyful songs will drive out every sorrow from your heart. And then anyone who comes in contact with you will sense My manifest presence, because your songs will have cleared the path. So sing for those who cannot sing for themselves! See this as a great weapon of intercession to drive back the enemy as well as to set the captives free! As a key opens a lock, watch how your freely abandoned song to Me will open the prison doors for everyone that is oppressed around you. So use this new-found key in total freedom and with great joy! Let your heart be lifted up as you go about My kingdom, bringing much freedom and great release to the captives. Sing in the Spirit, and also sing with your own understanding. Singing just as a little child would to Me, for it is not quality I desire, it is obedience!

And whatever you do, in word or deed, do everything in the name of the Lord Jesus, giving thanks to God the Father through Him (Colossians 3:17).

FLY WITH ME

I do not want you to be burdened down with the cares of this world. I have given you a new life and a conscience free from sin. So I want you to change your attitude to one of faith in My ability, not one of sorrow in your own perceived lack. Whose goodness do you wish to live in, Mine or your own? Whose righteousness is truly righteous? Mine, of course! Be done with fishing around in My sea of forgetfulness! Let your mind rise to a new level of faith. Put on My whole armor, and keep it firmly in place. Let your gratitude soar to new heights in Me. By My own hand I am able to deliver anyone who comes to Me in faith. I am the Truth! I am able to set at liberty all those who will believe. You have been given the free will to make choices in every area of your life. I will be glad to help you make any decision if you will only ask Me. Rest now, little one, and let Me have those things that are pressuring you to perform. Come fly with Me, and experience My freedom today. Fly – be free!

He Himself bore our sins in His body on the tree, that we might die to sin and live to righteousness. By His wounds you have been healed (1 Peter 2:24).

I AM THE RESTORER

Rest, and while you are resting, I want you to realize that I am right here holding you close to My heart. So snuggle down deep in My loving arms, and let Me soothe away every weight and whisk away every care. Let My nurturing heart of love minister to your deepest needs today; just stop and let Me love you! There is no "ought" or "should" here in My presence, only pure relief and holy joy - enough to fill every tired hurting place in your heart and abundantly more to share with those who cross your path. So sink down deeper still into the refuge of My manifest presence, and let Me love you back to life and peace. I am the restorer of the streets to walk in. But first you must receive Me as your restoration in every area of your life. On every level in which My healing touch is needed, I will be for you, personally, more than enough!

Come to Me, all who labor and are heavy laden, and I will give you rest. Take My yoke upon you, and learn from Me, for I am gentle and lowly in heart, and you will find rest for your souls. For My yoke is easy, and My burden is light (Matthew 11:28-30).

DEEPER WATERS

Precious treasures are here, My child, laid up in heaven for you. Abundant riches of every description are yours for the taking. I have planned an enormous harvest of blessings for My faithful ones. Not that you have to start some type of works routine to deserve My gifts, no, not at all! My gifts are absolutely free of charge, bought and paid for by My own eternal love, which was demonstrated for you on Mount Calvary long ago. Nothing remains now except for you to simply receive all that I have in store for you. Just come and take what already belongs to you. It is your inheritance and there are no strings attached. Your believing heart and your open mind are the only keys you will need to unlock the joyful riches of My kingdom. It greatly delights Me to have you possess all that I have purchased for you with My very own life. So now, I want you to enjoy My gifts freely, and extravagantly share them with others as I lead you out into the deeper waters of My life.

For the Lord God is a sun and a shield; The Lord bestows favor and honor. No good thing does He withhold from those who walk uprightly (Psalm 84:11).

A NEW FACET

Your hope is built on nothing less than My precious blood and righteousness. Just as this old song declared, so it is also true in your life. You must not trust the sweetest frame, not even your own; just completely cling to My unchanging name. I am your Rock! I am your Refuge! I am all you will ever need here in this life and throughout all eternity. So be at peace here in My loving arms once again, and let Me soothe away all of your discomfort. I want your heart to rejoice in this very moment as you experience My presence in a more tangible way. Allow your faith to rise up to receive Me in a manner you have never before known. Simply surrender your own ideas of how you perceive Me, and let Me reveal a new facet of Myself to you today. A well-cut jewel has many sides in which to reflect light, yet My immediate presence has many more illuminating facets to reveal to your heart right now. Will you receive Me today in a new light, a new revelation? This new light that seems new to you, is just another reflection of Who I Am. Simply trust Me to reveal Myself to your waiting heart in a crystal clear manner.

Peace I leave with you; My peace I give to you
(John 14:27).

SIMPLY RECEIVE ME

Treasures await you here in My presence. The gifts of My Spirit are yours for the asking. Even if you do not know what to ask for by name, simply ask for the best gift for the moment. I know what you mean, and I am pleased to shower Myself out upon you for every need of the hour. My gifts are not just some pretty trinkets to be used and then put on a shelf to collect dust! Each gift of Mine is a part of My person, a demonstration of Who I Am. Healing is a manifestation of the out ray of the divine, because I am Jehovah Rapha, the Lord your healer. The same is true of all of My gifts; they are expressions of Who I Am. The very God of miracles is in your midst! The very Word of God flows through your prophecies. Trust Me now, little one, to be to you all that you will ever need. No good thing have I withheld from you. Surely, I will not withhold Myself from you, but I instead will lavish My gifts upon you in an ever more increasing manner. All that you need to do is simply receive Me.

For unto us a child is born, to us a son is given; and the government shall be upon His shoulder, and His name shall be called Wonderful Counselor, Mighty God, Everlasting Father, Prince of Peace (Isaiah 9:6).

THE GOOD FIGHT OF FAITH

Cast off all guilt for it does not come from Me. If it were a gift from Me, I would expect you to cherish it, but guilt and condemnation are never from Me. They are merely your feelings of failure and defeat. Our enemy has a field day when he can make you think you are less than perfect. When you feel worthless or unworthy, it is because you are concentrating on the negative. This negativity is not faith, love, or any fruit of My Spirit. So rise up now in your most holy faith, and be done with the lesser attitudes. I know it is a battle within your mind and the environment around you. This is where the good fight of faith is most effective, right in your own backyard; right here where you live in your day-to-day, everyday routine. Let Me show you how to rise above these negative powers with My life-giving joy and peace-producing authority. The keys are in your own mouth, for it is the praising saint that walks above, and it is the worshiping one who rises to the place of safety and freedom, far away from the tyrant of guilt.

I will praise the name of God with a song; I will magnify Him with thanksgiving (Psalm 69:30).

YOUR BURDEN BEARER

Take a deep breath here in My presence and relax. It is not your responsibility to set the whole world right. Just simply come as a little child, climb up onto My lap, and ask Me to fix whatever needs fixing. The government of your life is upon My capable shoulders. So let go of the frustration and pressure to perform, and let Me have full control. The tension you store up pushes you away from My peace. So stop right now, and reevaluate what you are feeling and what you believe. Do not go another step carrying burdens that only I am capable of bearing. Please remember, I came to give to you My abundant life and be your burden bearer. Will you let Me do this for you today, and will you relinquish to Me everything that robs your joy and steals your peace? Trust Me now, and watch what I can do with whatever you give Me to fix. Expect a miracle, and if you truly believe, you will receive it now!

Now may the Lord of peace Himself give you peace at all times in every way. The Lord be with you all (2 Thessalonians 3:16).

BANNER OF VICTORY

My mercy extends to all generations; it reaches backward as well as forward. You have made a stand, here in your generation, to be My disciple; and being surrendered to Me, you have a right to claim your ancestry as well as your prodigy for My kingdom. As you stand in faith for all of those who belong to you, plant your banner of victory deep in the soil of My love, and let it wave freely for all to see. As an encouragement, remind them that My banners are used in wartime to rally the troops and give hope in the midst of battle, as well as to wave the message of victory for all to see. Remember the song, "Joy is the flag flown high from the castle of My heart when the King is in residence there – So, let it fly in the sky, let the whole world know, let the whole world know, let the whole world know – So, let it fly in the sky, let the whole world know that the King is in residence there." I am here and we are victorious, past, present, and future!

Therefore, as you received Christ Jesus the Lord, so walk in Him, rooted and built up in Him and established in the faith, just as you were taught, abounding in thanksgiving (Colossians 2:6-7).

PURSUE ME FULL-TIME

Life, liberty, and the pursuit of happiness are constitutional rights written by your forefathers to assure your well-being. Where do you think they got that idea? Yes, of course, only I can truly give life and liberty! But what about that last statement: the pursuit of happiness? Do you really believe that I want you to be happy? Many well-meaning ones have preached against that notion. What do you think the abundant life that I died to give to you really means? Could it really be true that I would want you to be happy? The opposite of happiness is sadness, and it is the desire of our enemy to make you sad and keep you there in one form or another. So if you really think about it and then truly believe My Word, you can grab a hold of happiness as a gift of My love. You should never let it go, no matter what the enemy throws your way. If you will pursue Me full-time, then happiness will always be the result. In My presence there is truly fullness of joy, and at My right hand there are always pleasures forevermore.

The Lord is My strength and My shield; in Him My heart trusts, and I am helped; My heart exults, and with My song I give thanks to Him (Psalm 28:7).

MY DELIGHT AND JOY

Dance, little one, dance with total abandon and simple delight in Me. As a child who is thrilled with a new toy squeals with joy, so let your gladness resound in freedom. Do not take anything for granted, because it will rob you of the pleasure of your discovery. If you keep your heart turned toward Me in true gratitude, then you will be able to experience My delight and joy in a more profound manner. So stop struggling, trying to keep everything in control. I am not telling you to be reckless, foolish, or undisciplined. I desire you to be child-like enough to simply enjoy the blessings of being Mine! Right now, take a deep breath and just smile. Close your eyes, and feel how good it is just to smile at Me! Can you see Me smiling at you? I am you know, and I am delighting in My very special creation – YOU! Can you see the flame of My love leaping with joy because of your nearness? Come closer yet, and let Me show you how I really feel about you as we dance our dance of love together this day.

You have turned for me My mourning into dancing; You have loosed My sackcloth and clothed me with gladness, that My glory may sing Your praise and not be silent. O Lord My God, I will give thanks to You forever! (Psalm 30:11-12)

EXTEND MY FORGIVENESS

Set your mind and heart in My direction, and you will find yourself walking in love and extending forgiveness everywhere you go. It does not work the other way around; you cannot walk in love or extend forgiveness in your own strength. If you will seek after Me first and foremost, with all of your heart and soul, you will be able to love and forgive freely without a struggle. It is a matter of looking higher and calling upon My ability, not relying on your own. Let peace be your umpire and determine the direction that you will take today. Now rise up in your most holy faith and make the choice to be forgiven and to extend My forgiveness. I want you to see that even when the opportunity arises, it will not be your forgiveness that you give to another, but Mine! You have no forgiveness of your own to give; yet you are privileged to extend Mine! If you see it this way, it will be much easier for you to participate in the forgiving process. Remember, it is no longer you that lives; it is I living within you, and the life you now live, you live by faith in Me, because it was I who gave Myself for you. Is this your confession today?

We love because He first loved us (1 John 4:19).

GOLDEN RAYS OF SILENCE

Do not let the silence frighten you, little one. I want you to receive it as a gift from My heart to yours, and let it minister to the deepest part of you by embracing it fully. Let My life-giving waves of love roll over you, right now, here in the silence of our retreat. Do not let your mind be filled up with plans or concerns; just give those to Me for safe keeping, and take what I am offering to you right now. This is a life-giving, freedom-making, and faith-producing moment to treasure. I will take care of you; I am your provider. I am the one responsible to look after all of your needs. You can rest assured that every little detail of your life has My full attention. Just make up your mind once and for all that you will not let the temporal be of more importance than the eternal. Then come and fly with Me, high above all the earthly cares, into the golden rays of silence where we can commune in freedom and with great joy, together once again.

And He said, "My presence will go with you, and I will give you rest (Exodus 33:14).

COMPLETE SALVATION

Trust Me, little one, to be for you all that you could ever want or need: your Lover, your Friend, your King, and your God - these and much more shall I be to you. Many have desired to know Me in a more intimate way, yet recoiled when I began to reveal Myself to them. It is your spirit that can receive the deeper revelations of Who I Am, not your flesh! Keep this in mind as we journey on together: the Spirit gives life; the flesh profits nothing. I am not saying that your body is fleshly and therefore cannot profit by My touch. This is an old religious notion that somehow the body is evil while the spirit is good. No, this is not true for I made you to be spirit, soul, and body. Each has its function, and each has its own need that I delight to take care of generously. So then, set aside your old nature; reckon yourself – your flesh – to be dead to sin. Then receive your new nature, spirit, soul, and body to be fully alive in Me. Now come to Me with great expectation, knowing that I will not disappoint you, and that I will be to you complete salvation in every area of your life.

There is no fear in love, but perfect love casts out fear.
For fear has to do with punishment, and whoever fears
has not been perfected in love (1 John 4:18).

A STOREHOUSE OF WONDER

Relax now in My presence. Let all worry and anxiety melt away here in My loving arms of assurance and provision. I will take care of all of your needs according to My riches here in heaven. Take courage, knowing that I have already fought and won the war for you. I have taken everything away from our enemy, and I have already given it all to you. Will you set your sights higher and believe that what I have accomplished, I have done for you to enjoy? Just like picking ripe fruit from a tree, so it is in My kingdom. You do not have to struggle about whether the earth's abundance is meant for you to receive; you simply take what you desire and enjoy it. So come even closer to Me now, and receive all that I have laid up in store just for you! I have a storehouse of wonder put aside for each of My children. Will you let Me lavish My gifts upon you today? Will you receive your very heart's desire from My hand, right now? I love you even more than you could ever imagine!

"Be still, and know that I am God. I will be exalted among the nations, I will be exalted in the earth"
(Psalm 46:10).

CHAPTER FIVE

God of All Mercies

I AM MERCY PERSONIFIED

Let all of the memories of past hurts and failures be washed away here in My cleansing, healing love. I am the God of all mercies, and I extend Myself to you anew this day. Mercy is not just a something that you receive from Me, but a Someone, because I am Mercy personified. I offer you Myself in a deeper, more intimate way, each time you ask for My mercy. When you seek to have a more insightful revelation of Who I Am, just ask for more of My mercy to be made manifest to you. This will keep you in a humble attitude, and thus, you will be able to receive more readily from Me. It is My merciful heart that sees your needs, and even before you ask Me to help you, I am already at work bringing the answers to you. So open wide your heart, and let Me fill you with more of My compassionate nature. Rest assured that My mercy is more than adequate, for every situation and circumstance that you find yourself faced with today. I, Mercy, will always find a way to be expressed to you!

So whatever you wish that others would do to you, do also to them, for this is the Law and the Prophets (Matthew 7:12).

117

A MOST FAVORABLE MANNER

I am for you right now, your haven, sanctuary, and refuge. Come take advantage of our relationship and enjoy resting here awhile with Me. Listen deeply, here in the quiet of My love, and hear My voice saying "Peace be still" to all of the troubled waters of your life. Let your soul bask in the sunshine of My personal love for you. Allow yourself to relax in mind and body as you drink deeply of My affection for you. There is no need to try to work up any religious duties. Simply be My child and receive what I have to give to you today. Remember that the government of your life is upon My capable shoulders and that I am well able to orchestrate all of the details concerning you in a most favorable manner. You are My bride, My beloved, and I want you, even here on earth, to enjoy this exalted status with all of its benefits in every area of your life. Will you allow Me to bless you right now? Will you simply receive and enjoy Me today?

Are not five sparrows sold for two pennies? And not one of them is forgotten before God. Why, even the hairs of your head are all numbered. Fear not; you are of more value than many sparrows (Luke 12:6-7).

118

ENCOUNTER MY PRESENCE

Divine revelation is My gift to you. Your desire to know Me more intimately is truly a blessing to Me. It is a holy and lovely request and one that I have already granted to you. So now, I want you to expect to meet with Me at every turn. Look for Me to manifest Myself to you throughout all of your life. I want you to expect to be made aware of Me in your work as well as your rest. I want to show you how to really live to the fullest in every area of your existence. My desire is for you to encounter My presence throughout your whole day, even in the smallest of things. So focus on Me, because I am everywhere present! Let Me open your eyes today as well as your heart, and allow Me to reveal Myself to you as you have desired. Will you trust Me anew today in this our greatest adventure? Can you believe that I will not withhold any good thing from you? All you have to do is simply ask Me to help you believe, and I will surely do it! I am right here, right now, loving you!

And God is able to make all grace abound to you, so that having all sufficiency in all things at all times, you may abound in every good work (2 Corinthians 9:8).

MY OVERSHADOWING PRESENCE

It will be a day of great joy in discovering My presence if you will allow Me to reveal Myself to you in the here and now. My glory is all around you, little one; you are engulfed with the out ray of the divine. I am right here deep inside of you as well as encircling you completely. Many can see My radiance when they look at you. Some will be aware of Whom it is that they are encountering when they come in contact with you, and some will not; yet this does not hinder My power and ability. If you keep your heart open and believing in My loving, healing presence, then My power will flow through you without a struggle. You can just relax and let it happen. Do you remember how I overshadowed Mary and she conceived? Come and discover what My overshadowing presence in you will bring forth today. My overshadowing presence will be great, and I will bless you and make you a blessing to the nations!

Let the word of Christ dwell in you richly, teaching and admonishing one another in all wisdom, singing psalms and hymns and spiritual songs, with thanksgiving in your heart to God. And whatever you do, in word or deed, do everything in the name of the Lord Jesus, giving thanks to God the Father through Him (Colossians 3:16-17).

I SEE BEYOND

Just settle back here in My arms of love, and let My peace wash over you right now. You do not need to perform any duty for Me to be pleased with you, as you already please Me by simply being who you are. I am pleased with you because you are My creation, and I created you for My own pleasure. So let all of the hurry, scurry, or any frantic striving melt away here in My presence. Take another drink of the nectar of My life-giving, life-sustaining power, and simply let Me love you as you are. Sometimes you wish you were more of this and less of that, but I delight in the person you are right now! I see beyond the entire pretense and all of the pain, deep into your longing, needy heart. Now is the time to let yourself be honest with Me. I want you to put aside anything that hinders you from freely coming to Me. My arms are open wide to receive you; My blessings are here waiting for you to claim for your own. Will you let Me love you today? Will you simply come to Me now and just be with Me?

Blessed are the peace makers, for they shall be called sons of God (Matthew 5:9).

ABOVE ALL ELSE

When your mind is busy and rushing in many directions, it is hard to concentrate on the one thing that is the most important. What is that one thing which is your heart's desire today? Is it something or someone? What has captured your attention above all else today? Can you hear Me saying Martha, Martha, you are troubled about many things, yet only one thing is needful, and Mary has chosen the best, which is simply to sit at My feet and learn of Me? Do you really know personally, for yourself, that My yoke is easy and My burden is light? Shake yourself loose now from all condemnation that tries to push or pull you in any direction, and take the other path that leads to My throne of grace. Just come running with all of your passion into My presence, knowing I am always here waiting for you. Who shall I call you today, Mary or Martha? The choice is yours as always, but My desire is that you would have a merry-Mary heart in the midst of a Martha, Martha world!

Humble yourselves, therefore, under the mighty hand of God so that at the proper time He may exalt you, casting all your anxieties on Him, because He cares for you (1 Peter 5:6-7).

MY TRUE HUMILITY

I Am the Almighty, All Powerful, All Knowing, and the Everywhere Present God! Is there anything too hard for Me? No, of course not! If it were not for My mercy, every living thing would be consumed in the fire of My purifying presence. There is no righteousness apart from Me! Every person's self-righteousness is as a filthy rag before Me and something to be burned or thrown away. Therefore, you can see why in the story I told of the Publican and the Pharisee that only the one who humbled himself and cried out for My mercy was justified. He went away just as if he had never sinned! The self-righteous one remained in his sin, no matter how right he proclaimed himself to be, because there is none righteous, no not one! The sooner My children become more deeply acquainted with My true humility, the more of My joy and freedom will be experienced. I resist the proud but I give grace to the humble. Will you receive My unmerited, unearned favor today? Will you sit at My feet and learn of Me? I am lowly and humble of heart, and you will find rest in Me for your soul.

And a harvest of righteousness is sown in peace by those who make peace (James 3:18).

EXPRESSIONS OF WHO I AM

Shake off any feelings that try to pull you into confusion and frustration, then come closer to Me and let Me infuse your heart and soul with My joyful peace. There is no one and there is nothing that can take away these, My gifts to you, unless you allow it, for I never want you to be without either one. This dynamic two-some, joy and peace, are a part of your weapons of warfare; they will see you through any land mine of hatred or fear. My peace will guide you, and My joy will strengthen you in every area of your life. They will also point the way for others who are seeking to find My kingdom. This is the light to be lifted up for all of the world to see: My peace, which passes all understanding, and My joy that is unspeakable and full of glory. These will sustain you for they truly are expressions of Who I Am: the Prince of Peace, and the embodiment of Joy itself.

If then you have been raised with Christ, seek the things that are above, where Christ is, seated at the right hand of God. Set your minds on things that are above, not on things that are on the earth. For you have died, and your life is hidden with Christ in God. When Christ who is your life appears, then you also will appear with Him in glory (Colossians 3:1-4).

A DEEPER REALITY

Your hungry heart will put other things aside and seek out a place to be alone with Me. I am always everywhere present, and so it is not as difficult to find Me as some of My children think. You need not wait on a feeling to know that I am near, because I have given you the gift of faith to exercise. Instead of begging Me to come from somewhere, simply realize that I am already here, and begin to talk to Me with that fact in mind. Do not wait for some sensation of confirmation to begin communicating with Me. I want you to live in the awareness of My immediate presence at all times, and this you can only do by faith. You are having a relationship with Me, for I am your living personal God. No religious duty could ever satisfy your soul; it only leads to weariness and disillusionment. So now, draw closer to Me by exercising your faith, and then I will allow you to experience a deeper reality of My ardent love and unending affection for you personally.

And He said to her, "Daughter, your faith has made you well; go in peace, and be healed of your disease"
(Mark 5:34).

MANIFEST FULFILLMENT

Trust Me, My little one, to be to you all that you will ever need. I am right here, loving you at all times. Just stop what you are doing, and let yourself fully realize Who it is that is speaking to you right now. Is there anything too hard for Me? Of course not! Not only do I want to help you in every area of your life, but I also desire to help others through you. I am your strength, and I want to flow in intensity through you to a hurting, dying world. I want to heal you and to satisfy others with My healing touch. I desire to speak to you, as well as speak through you, to encourage others and to set the captives free. You need not beg Me to do what I am already busy doing. Instead, begin to thank Me for all things by faith, and soon your belief will be turned to vision and then your vision will be turned to manifest fulfillment. I want you to experience the reality of My power even more than you desire to receive it. Will you say yes to Me now? Will you let Me love you and then love others through you today?

And His name – by faith in His name – has made this man strong whom you see and know, and the faith that is through Jesus has given the man this perfect health in the presence of you all (Acts 3:16).

A BLESSING TO MY EARS

Do not look back in shame or regret, because I have covered your past with My forgiving blood. Neither do I want you to concentrate on the future, for it is not yet, so leave it here in My capable hands. What you have is this present moment in time to use as you see fit. Whatever you decide to do with this time will affect your future in many ways. So live well and do good today but most of all enjoy your journey. Let nothing rob you of the joy I have personally given to you, as it is your strength and will carry you up above all of the pressures of your day-to-day life. Let songs of joy arise from within your heart to be a blessing to My ears. The words are not as important as the intent behind them so sing in the Spirit, and sing with your understanding also. Simply let My joy overflow your heart and bring to you the strength that I have intended for you to experience. Unspeakable joy, full of glory joy, here in My presence is the fullness of joy for you! So, will you come and partake of this cup of the new wine here with Me today?

I will bless the Lord at all times; His praise shall continually be in My mouth (Psalm 34:1).

IT WAS MY IDEA

Every time you speak to Me, I hear you! I want you to believe that your prayers are always welcome here; you can never ask of Me too much! It is My great desire to give to you all that you could ever need and even more besides. It was My idea to have you present your request to Me. I was the One who instructed you to ask, seek, and knock. As you are obedient to ask, you will receive, and as you obey Me to seek, you will find! Whenever you knock, because I have told you to do so, the door will be opened for you. I want you to know that these requests of Mine are for you to exercise in obedience. I want you to ask of Me, and then I will grant you your heart's desire in answer to your request. I want you to participate in My divine plan, and in order for Me to implement My plan in the earth, I need you to ask and receive. I want you to seek and find. I desire that you would also knock and then experience the doors of heaven opening to you. I long to pour out blessings upon you so large that you do not even have room enough to contain them. Will you be obedient to Me now; will you ask of Me today?

And My God will supply every need of yours according to His riches in glory in Christ Jesus (Philippians 4:19).

MY WISDOM AND DIRECTION

It is never too late to turn around and go in another direction. When you discover that the path you are traveling upon is in error, you can simply turn your heart and mind toward My loving presence, and then I can help you to turn around and go the other way. You do not need to repent from only big mistakes or huge sins; any misdirection can be rectified if you will humble yourself enough to let Me help you go back to your appointed route. Do not let shame take a hold of your mind, even for a second, because shame is always connected with pride. You were never meant to walk this life's path alone. You will always need My wisdom and direction in every area. It is My good pleasure to lavish your heart with all of the insight necessary for every situation if you will only ask Me for it. Now, will you ask Me for the help and the wisdom that you will need today? If you will, you can expect to experience a surge of My life-giving, life-sustaining presence, lifting your consciousness and directing your steps to be able to walk in My joy and peace today!

Abide in Me, and I in you. As the branch cannot bear fruit by itself, unless it abides in the vine, neither can you, unless you abide in Me (John 15:4).

A SINGLE RED ROSE

It is never a waste of time to come apart and be alone with Me. In the very act of your coming to Me, I am rushing to meet with you at the exact same time. I have so very much that I want to share with you that you could never exhaust My desire to give to you in abundance. I already know what you need; however, I still want you to ask Me to supply all of your needs as well as your wants. You could never ask too much! I have already laid up in store for you super abundantly more than you could ever ask or think. Right now, I just want you to enjoy My nearness. I want you to put everything else aside for awhile and just be here with Me. This is not a ritual that demands you to perform in order to get My attention. Come as you are, rest your head here on My breast, and let Me show you what My vision is for you. As you would receive a single, red rose, admiring its rich color, feeling its soft texture, and smelling its luscious scent, then please just so, receive Me today, as I always receive you, MY precious little rose!

Fear not, little flock, for it is your Father's good pleasure to give you the kingdom (Luke 12:32).

THE FATHER OF LIGHTS

The power of My blood is upon you; it covers and protects you every moment of every day in ways you have not yet recognized. Never underestimate the awesome authority under which you live in Me, My child. I am the One Who spoke the worlds into existence. All things are held together by the power of My spoken Word. Trust Me to be to you all that you will ever need. There is not anything that I am not able to perform on your behalf. Do not trouble yourself by worrying in any area; leave it all in My hands, and watch with delight and expectation as I undertake in your arena. Now settle back here in My arms, and let Me restore and refresh you. Will you receive what I have to offer to you right now? Do you want Me to be a father to you... not just a father... your Father - the Father of Lights? I Am already your Father, but will you let Me Father you right now? There is a vast difference between just the title and the actual experiencing of our Father and child relationship. So, again, I ask you, will you let Me Father you today?

The Lord your God is in your midst, a mighty one who will save; He will rejoice over you with gladness; He will quiet you by His love; He will exult over you with loud singing (Zephaniah 3:17).

I AM THE TRUTH

You shall know the Truth, and the Truth shall make you free. As you stick close to Me, you will know Me even better than you have before. It is not just knowing things about Me that causes our relationship to blossom, it is in knowing Me personally, intimately, face-to-face, day in and day out. Is this your heart's desire? It certainly is Mine! I am the Truth who has made you free. Think back to when we first met. Were you in more darkness and bondage then? Have you come into a measure of light and freedom because of knowing Me? Yes, you have, and you will continue to be ever more increasingly and daily enlightened, by My abiding presence within. You will taste of the exceeding abundance of My freedom on a continual basis by simply abiding in Me. By making your home in My heart, I am making My home in yours. We are one, and you shall experience all that this wonderful oneness entails, including knowing Me as the Truth personified. If you are ready, I am willing and able to reveal Myself to you as the Truth you are seeking right now!

He only is My rock and My salvation, My fortress; I shall not be shaken (Psalm 62:6).

HEAVEN ON EARTH

Treasure our time together right now, little one. It is indeed a wonderful time of healing and restoration just for you. Even though I am no respecter of persons, I do honor all those who come to Me of their own free will. I am so blessed that you have chosen Me above all else to be your Lord. You could have chosen anyone or anything to worship, yet you have chosen Me, which is truly the wisest choice you could ever make. Could you think that because you have chosen Me, there just might be a reward, and is this a surprise to you? Well, I want My secrets to be known to you, and I desire for you to experience My reward now. I know you have been taught to look forward to a heavenly reward, but I want you to experience heaven on earth right here, right now! Will you receive My gift to you today? You do not have to struggle or be under pressure; just say yes! A simple yes and thank you will do on your part, and I will be glad to reward you openly today.

For truly, I say to you, if you have faith like a grain of mustard seed, you will say to this mountain, `Move from here to there,` and it will move, and nothing will be impossible for you (Matthew 17:20).

FREEDOM IS MY BATTLE CRY

Healing and liberty are a part of My covenant of love with you. These are not only your wishes, but they are My desires for you and the whole world. Freedom is My battle cry for all of My children. Your health and wholeness are why I took those stripes upon My back. I allowed Myself to be beaten in order to secure your healing from every disease and torment. Whatever is making you uneasy is a dis-ease that I am standing against on your behalf even now. What I did for you was not a theory; it is indeed a reality! You have a right as My child to make a claim upon all that I have purchased for you. When I redeemed you at Calvary, I bought you for Myself. I paid the full price for your redemption, and that includes your health and welfare. You were a slave to sickness and sin, but I purchased you to set you free from all bondage. So rejoice now, and receive all that I have done for you. Just take what you need and be at ease. This is your day of healing and liberation!

O Lord My God, I cried to you for help, and You have healed me (Psalm 30:2).

BRING IT TO ME

I want you to stop being so hard on yourself. Stop judging and criticizing yourself! This may not be a conscious fault; it might be deeper like an inside, constant, quiet nagging. I want you to arrest those thoughts and refuse to entertain them. I love you, and I am for you, not against you. I desire that your inner, deeper thoughts be a blessing to you also. These pre-programmed messages are not from Me. They are lies and should be thrown out completely. Let Me re-program your heart and mind with the truth of My constant, abiding, eternal love for you personally. Let Me wash away all of the pain here in My healing arms of love. As you capture each negative thought, bring it to Me, and I will remove it and replace it with the truth. It is in knowing the truth that you are being set free continually. I am the Truth, and My words are Spirit and they are Life, bringing healing and wholeness to every area of your existence. So, will you give Me all that is pressuring you today? Will you bring it all to Me now?

And behold, a leper came to Him and knelt before Him, saying, "Lord, if you will, you can make me clean." And Jesus stretched out His hand and touched him saying, "I will; be clean." And immediately his leprosy was cleansed (Matthew 8:2-3).

UNTO ME

Gather up all of the fragments of your life and bring them here to Me. In My economy there is nothing ever wasted - even all of the little bits and pieces that seem insignificant to you are really the jewels in My treasury. I do not want you to overlook a single one of them for much can be learned from the smallest little seed. Do not disregard the very mundane and even routine parts of your life. These are also My gifts of stability for you to cherish. The little quiet moments are as important as your most productive hours, sometimes even more important. Let each word and every phrase be an expression of your love for Me, not just the words spoken to Me or about Me, but those also spoken to others. I want you to see your whole life as being lived out before Me in liberty and truth. Each and every gesture of the act of your love directed toward others is as sweet fragrant incense unto Me. Remember, when you have done it unto the least of My children, you have done it unto Me!

Truly, truly, I say to you, whoever believes in Me will also do the works that I do; and greater works than these will he do, because I am going to the Father (John 14:12).

CHAPTER SIX

Actively Pursue Me

THE FULLNESS OF FAITH

What is it that you want to hear Me say to you today? Do you need My direction or comfort? I am not asking you because I do not know what you need. My questioning you is to jar your attention to search your own heart and mind so that you might put yourself into a more receptive mode. I want you to come to Me as a little child full of confidence and open to receive all that you ask of Me. Remember, it is the askers who will receive, the seekers who will find, and those who knock who will have everything opened up for them. Those who actively pursue Me shall be rewarded here in this lifetime, as well as on out into eternity. So take some time to evaluate just what is most desirous to you right now. Then come and ask Me to help you to fulfill your dreams. It may not even be a full vision yet, just a hope in your heart, but let Me bring that hope into the fullness of faith. I love to satisfy My children with good things so please ask of Me. I am waiting to respond. Are you expecting to receive?

Let not your hearts be troubled. Believe in God; believe also in Me. In My Father's house are many rooms. If it were not so, would I have told you that I go to prepare a place for you (John 14:1-2)?

139

THE HIGHER LIFE

Repentance is the first order of the day. It is not just feeling sorry for missing the mark; it is a conscious, definite turning away from whatever has held you captive. By turning first to Me, you then have the power to resist all temptation. To re-pent is to come back to the higher life, and to resume your position here in Me where you belong. Seated together with Me here in heavenly places, you will be able to see from My perspective. It is My eternal outlook that you need because the earthly temporal viewpoint will only keep you bound by its alluring appeal. So now, let Me take you higher than you have ever dreamed possible. Allow Me to show you how to really live with your feet firmly planted on this soil while your heart is deeply rooted in My heavenly places. It really is possible to be at peace and to live in joy every day of your life! So simply turn around; I am right here behind you, waiting to lift you up in My loving arms and carry you away into My higher life.

Set your minds on things that are above, not on things that are on the earth (Colossians 3:2).

A FRESH NEW START

I do not want you to compare yourself with anyone else! I have made you uniquely different from all others. I have created you to be My own special jewel to show forth My praise by reflecting My glory. If you compare yourself with another, it is because you are desirous of reflecting their glory, and since all glory really belongs to Me, this is impossible. At the root of all this comparison is jealousy, envy, and an ungrateful heart. If you are truly thankful for just who I have created you to be, there will be no need to compare yourself with another. This is a form of judgment against yourself by a critical spirit. All judgment and criticism of others is rooted in self-judgment and criticism, and if I do not condemn you, how can you hold such a harsh opinion of yourself any longer? It is time for a fresh new start, a fresh new opinion of your self today - one of love and acceptance and one of gratitude and thanksgiving for whom I have created you to be. You are Mine, and I love you just the way you are. Will you let Me teach you how to love yourself today?

For whoever does the will of My Father in heaven is My brother and sister and mother (Matthew 12:50).

SWEET COMMUNION

Rejoice and revel in My manifest presence. As you set your heart and mind to offer praise to Me, I rush to reveal Myself to you in a more tangible form. I come down over you and rest Myself upon you; just as My Spirit overshadowed Mary, so I overshadow you right now. You know that I am always here within you, yet as you choose to express your praise of Who I Am, then I delight in revealing Myself to you in a more manifest manner. It is the weight of My glory that you feel upon you now. Receiving this blessing from Me involves exercising your faith; so reach out now and simply receive Me in this deeper way. Stretch out your faith and take what I am offering to you for no good thing will I ever withhold from you My beloved. You are My precious treasure, and I love to lavish My gifts upon you. Will you receive more of Me today? I am right here to pour Myself out upon you; so drink deeply My beloved, and enjoy our sweet communion together.

Therefore, if anyone is in Christ, he is a new creation. The old has passed away; behold, the new has come (2 Corinthians 5:17).

JUST MINE

How long has it been since you simply sat in My presence and enjoyed My nearness? Do you always feel like you must be doing something to please Me? It is not true, you know, as I am already pleased with you. I created you for My own pleasure, and I do derive great pleasure from you. Just like smelling the fragrance of a flower and admiring its color, I always enjoy being near you. I love who you are right now, and I love who you will become as you grow up in Me. Yet, I am not in a hurry for you to move from one stage to another, because I am presently enjoying each phase and each new moment of your life. I am also experiencing contentment with you, and I want you to experience My contentment too. I do not want you to rush through your life always striving for the next plateau without enjoying the one you are on right now. Today will you just be with Me? Will you let Me love you right where you are right now? Will you agree to simply be Mine today? Just Mine! It is not that I do not want you to do anything, little one; I just want you to be able to enjoy all that you are and do as you do it with Me.

But, you, beloved, building yourselves up in your most holy faith, praying in the Holy Spirit (Jude 1:20).

THE REALMS ON HIGH

I want you to just be quiet for a moment and realize that I am really right here with you now. Let yourself settle down into the peace of My immediate presence. When you really know beyond all doubt that Almighty God is surrounding you, then all strife will fall away, and every struggle will cease to torment you. There is nothing too difficult for Me to repair, and nothing too hard for Me to fix. I will supply all of your needs according to My very own riches in glory. I love you with a love that transcends all understanding, and I choose to reveal My affection for you in this present moment. Come closer now; press in past everything that would try to distract you. I have so very much that I desire to reveal to you. All you need to do is say yes, and I will do all the rest. Saying yes to Me now is your act of surrender. This will carry you above the temporal to be able to soar with Me in the realms on high where we are seated together in heavenly places.

Therefore, since we have been justified by faith, we have peace with God through our Lord Jesus Christ (Romans 5:1).

EXPERIENCE MY FREEDOM

Shake off the despair that wants to attach itself to you. Do not let anything pull you down from your place of joy and praise. Remember, My presence goes with you, and I am the One who gives you rest from all of your labors. As much as you need a time of rest away from your physical labors, even so, and much more, you need a rest from all emotional stress. At the first sign of any unrest, call out to Me for deliverance. You do not have to put up with it nor try to appease it! You do not have to accept it or receive it any longer! You are free to rebuke all dis-order, dis-ease, and dis-unity. Anything, yes, and everything that is unlike My loving Spirit, you are to renounce and resist in My name. I am all of the strength you will ever need, and I continually give Myself freely to you. It is in your weakness that you can know My strength. So take courage now, and set yourself, mind and heart, to enjoy this day with Me, free from all struggle by letting yourself believe the truth. For it is only in knowing the truth that you will experience My freedom indeed.

For everyone who has been born of God overcomes the world. And this is the victory that has overcome the world – our faith (1 John 5:4).

MY PATH OF LIFE ETERNAL

It is never too late to begin to go in a new direction. You can start over right now, and I will show you how. If the path that you are on now is not taking you where you want to go, then stop and let us together rethink your plans. Let's look at the road map and determine the best route for you to take so that you can enjoy your journey and arrive safely at the appointed destination. Everything that you will need for clear direction is already written down in My Book of Life, and you can trust Me to be your guide all the way from earth to heaven. I will lead you each step of the way and will show you where to stop and rest, as well. I will point out the sights of interest, and I will warn you of all of the pitfalls along the way. I have not left you comfortless; I am right here with you, and I will never leave you, no never! So, rise up now, rejoicing as you allow Me to lead you through this journey of your lifetime. I am the Way, and I delight to show you My path of life eternal.

He was foreknown before the foundation of the world but was made manifest in the last times for the sake of you who through Him are believers in God, who raised Him from the dead and gave Him glory, so that your faith and hope are in God (1 Peter 1:20-21).

146

THE LOVE TEST

Love is Who I Am so love is all around you and deep within you right now! I am Love made manifest! I am Love incarnate! I am Love personified! I am not just a feeling or an emotion, but I do inspire both feeling and emotion. You know what scripture teaches about love: it is always patient, kind, longsuffering, and gentle, as well as good and faithful. It is not envious or boastful, not harsh, hard, sharp or pressing. Well, I want you to know that these are My very own characteristics. This is how I treat you, and if you are experiencing anything to the contrary, I want you to know that it is not from My Spirit. You can judge which spirit is influencing you by giving it the love test, and if something does not come from My Spirit of love, do not receive it; refuse to entertain it or give it a second thought. Simply turn your mind and heart back toward what love really is, and then you will be face-to-face with Who I really am – Love Eternal.

Finally, brothers, rejoice. Aim for restoration, comfort one another, agree with one another, live in peace; and the God of love and peace will be with you (2 Corinthians 13 :11).

LET ME CLEAR THE AIR

Forgiveness is a wonderful thing! It frees everyone concerned to enjoy the life that I have given. Each party is released to be all that I have created them to be. This is a spiritual matter, a gift of the highest order from My heart to yours. This is the reason I came to earth, to establish complete forgiveness, and when you forgive others, you are following in My footsteps. So do not let any time elapse before you begin the process whenever you find yourself hurt or offended in any way. Whenever that old, uneasy feeling starts to rise in your heart, bring it to Me immediately. You do not have to justify yourself before Me; I have already done that for you. You can be completely honest and above board. Simply present the whole matter to Me. Pour out your feelings just as they are to Me, and together we will extend our forgiveness to those in need. Be free now to get everything off of your chest, and let Me clear the air of any unforgiveness that might be in your own heart today.

Blessed be the God and Father of our Lord Jesus Christ! According to His great mercy, He has caused us to be born again to a living hope through the resurrection of Jesus Christ from the dead, to an inheritance that is imperishable, undefiled, and unfading, kept in heaven for you (1 Peter 1:3-4).

148

GRASP THE MAGNITUDE

Every day is a glorious day because I am alive! You, too, can really live forever in the power of My resurrection. I want you to focus all of your attention on just what My coming back from the dead to live forever more really means to you, personally. Yes, I arose for the whole of mankind - for the entire world - yet I came back to life also for you in particular. I want you to see the truth of this fact because I would have both died and resurrected just for you, alone. Even if you were the only person on earth, I would have done it all for you. I love you that much! I am alive right now for you. I am living eternally for you. Can you grasp the magnitude of this reality? No, of course not, not in your own understanding. But I am willing to give you all of the revelation that you desire if you will just ask Me. Trust Me now, My little one, to bring to you all of the benefits of My resurrection, salvation, healing, and deliverance. Will you let Me help you fully possess what I have purchased for you? I paid the highest price ever, because you were worth it all to Me.

Behold, God is My salvation; I will trust, I will not be afraid; for the Lord God is My strength and My song, and He has become My salvation (Isaiah 12:2).

LIFE-CHANGING MINISTRY

My divine healing power is at work in you right now. I am always repairing every part of your life. Think of it just as the ebb and flow of your breath. As you breathe in, My healing floods in and through every member and every cell of your spirit, soul, and body. As you breathe out, disease, pain, and disorder are expelled. It is My rhythm for I am constantly in motion, bringing life-giving energy in as well as carrying all harmful substances out of your life. I am living for you, right here inside of you, to not only heal you, but to be your health as well. You know these things in your mind, but today will you let Me reveal this knowledge to you at a deeper level? I desire to minister this truth to your heart as well as your body and especially to your mind, will, and emotions. Will you receive from Me today My life-giving and life-changing ministry? I want to touch you and make you whole in every area of your life. May I touch you right now?

For if, because of one man's trespass, death reigned through that one man, much more will those who receive the abundance of grace and the free gift of righteousness reign in life through the one man Jesus Christ (Romans 5:17).

TOP MOST PRIORITY

It is not wrong to come aside to sit and soak in My presence. It is a privilege! Sometimes you admire accomplishment and orderliness above communion and relationship. That is why you often struggle in taking the time to be personally refreshed by Me. The ease with which you are able to switch your focus reflects your true priorities. When it is hard to stop right in the middle of a project to steal away with Me for awhile, it just proves that you need to do it even more and to rethink your values. Is it your work or My presence that you desire more? Work is always good in its place, under My direction, but never as a replacement for our relationship. You cannot throw Me a token kiss and expect Me to be satisfied with second place. I will never be content with anything less than first place in your life, which should be your top-most priority. Will you allow Me to stir your desire for a deeper relationship with Me today, and come aside right now to simply be yourself with Me once again?

And He said to them, "Come away by yourselves to a desolate place and rest awhile." For many were coming and going, and they had no leisure time even to eat (Mark 6:31).

THE POWER OF MY BLOOD

There is not anything that is more powerful than My blood! It was shed for the remission of all sin. I carried it all the way to heaven to make the atonement for all inequity. My life is in My blood so it is eternally powerful. All disease and sickness must respond and cease to exist when My blood is applied. I want you to be aware of the authority I have given to you to call upon the power of My blood! I also want you to use My authority, and apply My blood as medicine to any wound. Come close now, and receive from My hand the very life-giving, life-sustaining force that you have need of today. Let Me sooth your tired nerves and heal all of your broken places. Allow Me to be all that you need and all that you desire today. I am closer to you than your very own breath. So drink in My presence just as you take in My broken body and My living blood. Come now, and let us commune together. My body will nourish you, and My blood will quench your thirst forever!

This was to fulfill what was spoken by the prophet Isaiah; "He took our illnesses and bore our diseases" (Matthew 8:17).

A CYCLE OF PERPETUAL CARE

Those precious ones who are on your mind and heart are there because they are on Mine. Not a moment goes by in all of life that any one of them is out of My reach. I am intimately acquainted with all of their requests and busy supplying all that they could ever need. The problem lies on the receiving end which is why I have instructed My children to preach the "good news," in order that all of My loved ones might know how much they are cared for and loved. Simply take from Me what is needed, not just once, or here-and-there, but freely and continually, with simplicity, receive all that I have laid up in store for the taking. Are you beginning to understand that there is nothing that is being withheld from you or anyone else? It is only a matter of your reaching out with your faith in Me, turned up to high power, and simply taking what I am continually showering down upon you. Then as you have freely received, you are to freely give. It is a cycle of perpetual care, because I love you!

Jesus Christ is the same yesterday and today and forever (Hebrews 13:8).

THE POSSIBILITIES ARE ENDLESS

Forget now the former things and lay it all down again at My feet. Let My peaceful presence wash over your heart and mind, and take into your body My healing virtue. I have come to give to you My abundant life, My very own overflowing, energizing, and full to the top life. It is eternal and present at the same time, because I AM everywhere, the past, present, and future. I am not limited to one time frame or one dimension so you can see the possibilities are endless as to what I can do in every area of your life. Even if you let your imagination soar, I am still beyond what you can conceive. I am still more powerful than you can begin to realize. So allow yourself to have a field day! Let all restraints fall off of your mind, and simply come ask Me for anything that your heart desires. If you can think it up, it can be accomplished. Let Me show you how to pray constructively and without the limits of an earth-bound attitude. Come fly with Me today above and beyond the temporal.

Then Jesus answered her, "O woman, great is your faith! Be it done for you as you desire." And her daughter was healed instantly (Matthew 15:28).

IN ALL OF MY GLORY

Love is the answer to every question! It is the first and most necessary response to any and every need. Love covers a multitude of sins. Love is kind and unselfish, easy to be entreated, and full of mercy and grace. It is neither self-reliant nor self-centered. Love is freedom in perfect manifestation. Love carries within itself the power to change the whole world. Love is not greedy or envious; it is giving and forgiving. Love is all you need, and it is Mercy personified because that is Who I Am. I am more than just a sweet feeling. Wisdom, power, and love - these words are all interchangeable because they are expressions of My Person. When you ask for wisdom, you will receive power and love; likewise, whenever you ask for love, you will receive wisdom and power. I do not just give you pieces of Who I Am; no, I have come to live inside of you in all of My glory. You have inherited the completeness of the Godhead bodily! So let your rejoicing begin, and today treasure all of the benefits again of My merciful, wise, and powerful presence within you.

Before they call I will answer; while they are yet speaking I will hear (Isaiah 65:24).

155

ALWAYS AVAILABLE

There are ways that seem to be right, yet they only lead to destruction. I want you to be aware that things are not always what they may appear. This awareness will help you bring everything before Me prior to making a final decision. I will help you to discern the truth in every matter if you will simply ask Me. I do not want you to be deceived about anything. I am the Truth and in Me, you are free. You are now liberated from all bondage, past, present, and future. Nothing can hold you back from My perfect will for your life. Because you have chosen to be Mine, I have given you the power to live in Me and in freedom on every level: spiritual freedom, mental freedom, and physical freedom. When you experience the contrary, resist it, knowing that it is not My highest will for you. My love for you lives continually, and My mercy is toward you forever. I want you to realize that My wisdom is always available to you; so will you simply ask Me for what you need right now?

And He called the twelve together and gave them power and authority over all demons and to cure diseases, and He sent them out to proclaim the kingdom of God and to heal (Luke 9:1-2).

AN ETERNAL FIRE

You have been set apart, My child, for Me exclusively. I have called you to Myself for My own personal pleasure. I enjoy your company and desire to be with you continually. No one and nothing else could ever take your place. You are Mine eternally, and I am yours forever! Everything I have is yours; do you believe that? I know it is hard to imagine, but it is the truth. I came to earth to claim you as My bride and to bestow all that I possess upon you. What I want in return is simply your love. I want to just be with you. I want to hold you close to My heart and tell you of My great love for you. It is truly unconditional and free, no strings attached. It is an all-consuming, ardent affection that nothing can ever quench - an eternal fire, always blazing bright and ever expanding to engulf all in its wake. My love for you covers, protects, heals, liberates, comforts, and provides. Will you come closer now and receive Me? Will you say yes to Me again today? When you say yes to Me, you are saying yes to love eternal.

And without faith it is impossible to please Him, for whoever would draw near to God must believe that He exists and that He rewards those who seek Him (Hebrews 11:6).

CHAPTER SEVEN

Gifts of Love

WISDOM WRAPPED IN MERCY

Wisdom is the principal necessity in your life! It should be your first request in every situation. I have already lavished all of My wisdom upon you so right now all you need to do is receive with an open heart and mind. Wisdom should also be your first prayer for others because wisdom is the primary need in every life. My wisdom and My mercy go hand in hand because these are both attributes of Who I Am. My desire for you is that you would now truly experience and enjoy My presence manifested as wisdom wrapped in mercy. It is in the purity and peacefulness of My wisdom that you will find rest. It is in the reception of My mercy that you will discover fulfillment in every area of your life. I want you to trust Me. Trust that I have your best interest at heart and that I am leading you on a path that I have created just for you. Let the excitement of this knowledge strengthen you today. These gifts of love are for you to enjoy and to share with others as I lead you.

Let us then with confidence draw near to the throne of grace, that we may receive mercy and find grace to help in time of need (Hebrews 4:16).

MY SPECIAL CREATION

When you call out to Me, I say, "Here I am!" Lay aside all thoughts that I might be somewhere else afar off. I am living right here inside of you right now, and I am not ever going to leave you. Ours is a forever relationship. No matter where we go, we are always together. You do not have to beg Me to show up when you feel you are in need, because I am more near to you than your very own breath. My life-giving force is flowing through your veins, bringing healing and restoration to every part of your life. I am continually renewing you in every area so look up, cheer up, rise up, and be in high spirits, because I am at work in you now, bringing My deliverance from all bondage. You can relax and enjoy the process, knowing that I will complete what I have started, and I will publish what I have authored. You are My special creation and I love taking care of you.

Looking to Jesus, the founder and perfecter of our faith, who for the joy that was set before Him endured the cross, despising the shame, and is seated at the right hand of the throne of God (Hebrews 12:2).

THE BANK OF HEAVEN

Our quiet time together is indeed a treasure house that few take time to enjoy. In a world of instant everything, many find it hard to stop and just reflect on what it really means to be My child. I am not trying to put a harsh demand upon you when I ask you to come aside for awhile and simply just be with Me. In reality, I desire to bless you in ways only found in quiet solitude with Me. I am not trying to take anything away from you; on the contrary, I am longing to give to you. A new sense of My peaceful presence awaits you here in My arms. A literal storehouse, full of My blessings, is yours for the taking. A deeper awareness of Who I Am and what it means to be loved by Me, all of this and so much more, is here in the bank of heaven already accredited to your account. Will you make a withdrawal today? Will you come and draw upon My passion to be a blessing to you personally today?

I will greatly rejoice in the Lord; My soul shall exult in My God, for He has clothed me with the garments of salvation; He has covered me with the robe of righteousness, as a bridegroom decks himself like a priest with a beautiful headdress, and as a bride adorns herself with her jewels (Isaiah 61:10).

I DESIRE INTIMACY

I am coming back to earth very soon now. It is not as important for you to be able to read all the signs of My imminent return as it is to be ready in your heart. Keeping your mind focused in My direction will help you stay prepared for that great and joyous day; however, knowing that I am right here inside of you now, by My Holy Spirit, will keep your mind at peace. Do not struggle to try to discern My will; simply come to Me and let Me reveal it to you. The bottom line is that I want you to be rejoicing at all times, no matter what it looks like, because I am always here with you. My desire is for you to be happy just because of My nearness. Let your contentment be established in Who I Am, not just in what I am able to do for you. Every good and perfect gift comes from Me, and it is good that you do appreciate them all. Yet, it is a better thing to have true appreciation for the Giver that I Am. I want you to know Me, not just things about Me. I desire intimacy with you. What do you desire of Me today?

Oh give thanks to the Lord, for He is good; for His steadfast love endures forever! (1 Chronicles 16:34)

THE POWER IS MINE

I want you to seek Me and My kingdom first! Yet, before you rush to try to accomplish My desire, I want you to experience for yourself Who I Am! Let Me reveal to you just what My kingdom is really all about. You know that I, and My kingdom, reside on the inside of you, but do you really know what My kingship is all about? Is your knowledge based on other people's opinion or on firsthand experience in accordance with My Word? Well, of course, I know the answers to My questions, so now, I am asking you personally: what do you really believe? I want to jar your attention out of any religious traditions that have kept you in bondage and held you back from My very best for you. Are you willing to let Me strip you of all your self-protecting ways? Self-righteousness and self-preservation are stumbling blocks that prevent you from fully enjoying My presence. In order to even enter My kingdom, you must come as a little child: open, honest, inquisitive, and teachable. If you are willing, I will do all the rest. The choice is yours, and the power is mine!

Jesus turned, and seeing her He said, "Take heart, daughter; your faith has made you well." And instantly the woman was made well (Matthew 9:22).

A HIGHER DIMENSION

As you cry out in the behalf of others, you are sowing seeds of kindness, of which you will reap a bountiful harvest. I want you to know that I have also set watchmen on the walls of your life, who cry out to Me for your safety and well-being continually. I have knit you together in a loving family, yet whether you know who they are or not is not the important thing. I have My loving ones all around the world who hear My voice and pray as I instruct them. It is not a matter of physical proximity or mental understanding. Prayer is a vehicle of My Spirit, and with Me there are no distance or time barriers. So jump into the river of My abiding love, and swim with Me into lands, as of yet, unknown to you. I will reveal the how and what of this thing called prayer. Let Me expand your sphere of influence in the spiritual realm today. Shake loose of all the limits imposed upon your mind, and come soar with Me to a higher dimension of a deeper revelation of Who I Am. I will teach you all that you will need to know. Are you ready to fly with Me?

Commit your way to the Lord; trust in Him,
and He will act (Psalm 37:5).

OUT INTO THE ETERNAL

Do not be shy or keep yourself back from My touch. I am delighted that you have chosen to come closer to Me now to sit at My feet and learn of Me. You could never spend too much time with Me for I always enjoy our time alone together. I always have new facets of Myself to reveal to your open heart. I have many sides of My character unknown to you, which I wish to disclose to you now. How much of My peace are you experiencing right now? If you will give Me all of your tension and concerns today, you can know Me as your Prince of Peace in a deeper sense. Come fly with Me above the temporal, out into the eternal, and let Me show you things beyond your natural mind, things of lasting quality! Simply relax and trust Me to be your Guide. It will be a mini-vacation, a true flight of fancy. All you need to do is present yourself as a living sacrifice to Me, and I will take care of the itinerary. Are you ready for the take-off?

Therefore let us leave the elementary doctrine of Christ and go on to maturity, not laying again a foundation of repentance from dead works and of faith towards God, and of instruction about washings, the laying on of hands, the resurrection of the dead, and eternal judgement (Hebrews 6:1-2).

IT HONORS THE CREATOR

I am your Redeemer; I have purchased you for Myself. I have created you to bring pleasure to My heart, and I re-created you in Myself to make it possible for you to be a blessing. You are a blessing to Me when you are freely expressing yourself in the truth. When you love yourself, it honors Me because when the created one appreciates the creation, it honors the creator! When you value a hand-made item, you give glory to its creator. In like manner, when you appraise yourself highly, it brings honor and glory to Me. Do you see the correlation? Think of the famous painters and composers: when their works are recognized, their names are exalted. Mankind is My highest and best creation, and when I came to rescue you, I re-created you in My own image and likeness. I love you, and I want you to love what I have made you to be. Will you let Me show you how to love yourself today?

I have been young, and now I am old, yet I have not seen the righteous forsaken or His children begging for bread (Psalm 37:25).

THE PURE AND HOLY ONE

Never hesitate to put aside the temporal in exchange for the eternal. Set your mind and heart on things above; this is where your true life resides, here at My right hand in the heavenly places. It is My gift to you to be able to see past the imminent and out into the realm of My Spirit. This will seem like uncharted territory to your natural mind, but I have charted it all long ago, and I will be your Navigator. So now bring every sense of guilt and condemnation to Me, and lay it all down here at My feet, as you do not need to carry those heavy burdens here in My presence. I have already died to release you from that bondage so today, please pick up your gift of My righteousness, and wear it proudly, showing off joyfully what I have already lavished upon you. I want you to experience the freedom I bought and paid for with My own life's blood. Today, will you cast off your consciousness of sin and unrighteousness? Then receive a new revelation of how I see you in purity and true holiness, because you are in Me, the Pure and Holy One.

Do not be anxious about anything, but in everything by prayer and supplication with thanksgiving let your requests be made known to God (Philippians 4:6).

MY COVENANT OF PEACE

I have come to illuminate all darkness, to liberate all who are bound, and to scatter seeds of kindness from the tree of life. I have also come to give you My confidence in every area of your life; not so that you would be prideful or have no need to ask Me for help, but in order for you to move through each situation of your life with ease and assurance. My desire is for you to live a stress-free life in the midst of a stressful world. I want your confidence and assurance to be based upon your relationship with Me and upon My covenant of peace that I have already given to you. My covenant of peace was written in My own blood on the cross of Calvary, and this is where I purchased your freedom and your health. This covenant is a sign of My everlasting love for you so take joy today from My well of salvation, and be assured that My constant care and provision will always be available to you. Today, will you draw upon our covenant in freedom with great expectation of My goodness?

Let us draw near with a true heart in full assurance of faith, with our hearts sprinkled clean from an evil conscience and our bodies washed with pure water (Hebrews 10:22).

170

I LOVE TO GIVE

Trust Me again, even here and now, to be to you all that you could ever need. I will supply you with whatever you need, and all that I require is that you come to Me and ask. You can never ask too much because My supply is endless and has no limit! Are you tired; do you need rest? Ask of Me! Are you hungry; do you need food? Ask of Me! Are you worried; do you have a difficult problem to solve? Ask of Me! There is no area where you experience need which is unacceptable to Me, so I want you to ask of Me and to ask largely. It honors Me when you put your trust and faith in My ability to supply what you need. I will not withhold any good thing from you so be bold, and let your imagination be free to roam through the possibilities of time and space, and see just what you can come up with to ask of Me today. This is to be a pleasure for both of us as I love to give good gifts to My children. What would you like to receive today?

For God so loved the world, that He gave His only Son, that whoever believes in Him should not perish but have eternal life (John 3:16).

A DEEPER LEVEL

My gifts and callings are permanent; I do not change My mind and take back what I have freely given to you. On the contrary, I increase and refine each gift to make them more efficient and useful. I also increase and refine you because you are a gift to Me. You have given yourself to Me freely and without reservation, just as I have given Myself to you. You are Mine forever just as I am yours for all eternity. Drink deeply now of My nearness, and let yourself enjoy our time together. Let all of your cares and concerns be put at rest here in My arms of love. Let Me wash over you with My cleansing, healing power. Allow Me to comfort and refresh your soul right now. Today we will take our relationship to a deeper level. It will be as if time is standing still; no pressure to perform will interrupt our reverie. Will you join Me on this journey of love and freedom? The rewards are out of this world!

He is the image of the invisible God, the first born of all creation. For by Him all things were created, in heaven and on earth, visible and invisible, whether thrones or dominions or rulers or authorities – all things were created through Him and for Him. And He is before all things, and in Him all things hold together (Colossians 1:15-17).

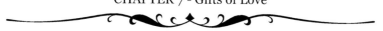

THE VERY HEART OF GOD

You, My little one, are precious to Me at all times, not just when you feel good about yourself or have some sense of worthiness, but every moment of every day you are a delight to My fatherly heart. I am glad that I created you just the way you are. I had an idea, and I set out to bring it to pass. That great thought was YOU! You are not a mistake or an accident; you were planned and conceived in the very heart of God! Now I want you to stop allowing yourself to fret about yourself. I want you to start appreciating yourself, and be thankful for every little detail of your existence. Shake loose now of every depressing thought, and rise up in your most holy faith by praying in your spiritual language. You will be praying according to My will and can be assured that My generous hand will supply all of your need. I love YOU, and I do have a great plan for YOUR life.

Rejoice always, pray without ceasing, give thanks in all circumstances; for this is the will of God in Christ Jesus for you (1 Thessalonians 5:16-18).

THIS VERY MOMENT

I want you to be still and very quiet here in My presence for awhile. I want to remove everything from your mind and heart that causes you pain. I want to abolish, right here and now, every guilty feeling and pressure from the evil force. If you will let Me, I will set you free to enjoy every aspect of your life. I do not want you to live in dread or fear of anything as these things only bring torment and bondage, none of which has ever come from Me. All of My gifts to you are liberating and can be passed on to others as a blessing. I want you to experience My freeing, life-giving presence this very moment. I want you to take your time and allow yourself to receive from Me. I have many gifts I want to bestow upon you and numberless blessings that I wish to impart into your expectant heart. Therefore, come away My beloved, and spend some time with Me. Come closer My beloved, and spend this time with Me.

And He is the head of the body, the church. He is the beginning, the firstborn from the dead, that in everything He might be preeminent. For in Him all the fullness of God was pleased to dwell, and through Him to reconcile to Himself all things, whether on earth or in heaven, making peace by the blood of His cross (Colossians 1:18-20).

TAKE A DEEP BREATH

This is the day that I have made, and I want you to rejoice and be exceedingly glad in it. Each breath you receive is a gift from My heart of love to you. I want your very own breath to be a constant reminder of My love and provision for you. I desire that you would be free to receive from Me and to give to others just as naturally as you breath in and breath out without any thought as to where the next breath is coming from. Just like your heart that is set on automatic pilot beats continually, so let your praise rise to bless My heart. If your mind is turned toward Me, then our communication will be a very natural, free-flow of give and take. So put on the garments of praise that I have woven just for you, and let your heart soar with Me today above all heaviness. Now today, take a deep breath, and let us continue on our journey together.

This is the day that the Lord has made; let us rejoice and be glad in it (Psalm 118:24).

HEART OF HEARTS

The force of My vision, down deep in your innermost being where the real you resides, is the essence of life. As you think in your own heart, so are you! It is deeper than your mere conscious mental capacities; it is in your subconscious where all true change takes place. In your heart of hearts, at the core of your being where I reside, is where your strength is found. This is where joy bubbles up from; this is where love dwells, and it is the control center of your life. If you will not lean upon your own understanding and will acknowledge Me in all of your ways, I will then direct your path in every area of your life. So bring to Me now all things that try to rob you of My peace, and just lay them all before Me. Let us begin now to sort them out to discover how they are disturbing your peace and just what thoughts in your heart may be responsible for this torment. You can trust Me to reveal the truth to you, and knowing the truth will set you free today!

So Jesus said to the Jews who had believed Him, "If you abide in My word, you are truly My disciples, and you will know the truth, and the truth will set you free" (John 8:31-32).

DIVINE RELATIONSHIP

Relax here in My arms once again. Cast every one of your cares upon My capable shoulders, and let Me carry all of the weights and concerns of your life. I delight to relieve you of every burdening care! You can ask Me for anything, and I will be glad to grant you your heart's desire. I Am your Master and Lord, and because of My great love for you, I have turned things upside down, which released you from being a load-carrying slave for I now carry your burdens. I, Love, also changed your name to friend and placed you in the seat of honor beside Me on My throne. You are seated together with Me right now here in heavenly places, far above all powers, principalities, and the rulers of this present darkness. You can rest assured that your placement here with Me is permanent! What I have done for you is eternal, and My gift to you is an abundant, free, and forever existence with Me. I want you to know that you are eternally living in a divine relationship with Me right now!

By faith we understand that the universe was created by the word of God, so that what is seen was not made of things that are visible (Hebrews 11:3).

JUST SAY YES

Listen very carefully; can you hear the song of the little bird? It sings because it was created to sing. I desired it to be so and it was! Generations after generation of songbirds have brought a great joy to My heart. Likewise, I created you to have fellowship with Me, to be My friend and companion, and I want you to know that you are a delight to Me continually. I love it when you seek Me out to be alone with Me, and I am thrilled when even in the midst of much activity your heart turns to Me in silent praise. I am blessed when in the press of many people you long for intimacy with Me alone. I promised to keep you in perfect peace if your mind was stayed on Me, and every opportunity that you have taken to be good to your brothers and sisters, I know you truly did it as unto Me. Rest here now in My love for you, and drink deeply of the wells of salvation for I desire to give you a gift today. Will you receive it? If so, just say yes!

Therefore, since we have been justified by faith, we have peace with God through our Lord Jesus Christ (Romans 5:1).

THIS BRAND NEW DAY

It is a brand new day; a day to let your spirit soar with great delight. I created this particular day just for you to enjoy. It is your day! Like a little child, I want you to face this and each new day with your heart wide open and your mind fixed on My immediate presence. Every day can be a new beginning if you will receive it as such. Put aside now all negative thoughts and worries, and plunge into this new day just as a swimmer dives deep into the water. So with full force and reckless abandon, jump into My arms right now, and I will catch you. I want you to see yourself jumping into My arms just like a little child would, and trust that I really will catch you! I love to reveal exciting new things to you and to watch your eyes light up with the discovery. Will you press into Me and experience My closeness right now? Let Me take you, this brand new day, on an adventure out into My fathomless billows of love!

I have set the Lord always before me; because He is at My right hand, I shall not be shaken (Psalm 16:8).

179

IN MY EMBRACE

You say and sing to Me that I am more than enough for you. I want you to think through your life, each aspect and every relationship, and one-by-one see if I am to you more than enough. Is this a statement of truth or just a nice idea? Is it your desire, or your reality; or have I become everything to you in every area? This is by no means a question of condemnation to cause you concern. To the contrary, it is a question, that if answered from your heart, and not from your mind, will bring great joy to you. I already know the answer, and the question is not for My information. It is for you to take some time and really search your own heart for the truth. No matter what you find there in your heart, know that I am pleased with you just as you are. I want you to enjoy the journey of finding all of your hopes and dreams met fully here in My embrace!

Cast your burden on the Lord, and He will sustain you;
He will never permit the righteous to be moved
(Psalm 55:22).

CHAPTER EIGHT

New Beginnings

BEGIN TO REJOICE

Just rest here in My arms of love awhile, and soak up all of the comfort and attention that your heart desires. Do not let anything or anyone crowd out our time together. Set aside the duties of the day, and place each person that is on your heart into My capable hands. Now trust Me to take care of each and every one, just as I have promised. Now, with great joy and expectation, begin to rejoice that I have heard your heart's cry and that I will do exceedingly, abundantly above all that you could ever even think to ask of Me. I delight to bless My children with good things continually. I watch over all of My creation and no one slips between My fingers. No, I hold each one close to My heart. Yet not everyone is aware of My constant love for them. They have been told lies to keep them in bondage by our enemy. However, the more you receive the truth from Me for yourself, the more able you become to proclaim it. Your boldness to share My love will increase as you take the time to come and simply receive all that you need from Me.

Beloved, let us love one another, for love is from God, and whoever loves has been born of God and knows God (1 John 4:7).

183

A MATTER OF TRUST

Now bring all of your needs to the altar of your heart where I live and rule as King. I am concerned about each and every one of your desires. Everything that touches you touches Me first, and I am genuinely touched with the feelings of all of your infirmities. You are not alone in any area of your life. Now, once again, I say bring all of your needs to Me; tell Me all about them in great detail. Even though I already know deeply how you feel, it is good for you to get it up and out of your mind and to talk it all over with Me. This not only helps you to release your burdens, it also makes room in your heart to receive My life-giving, sustaining power. So talk, shout, scream, and cry it all out as I hold you here in My arms of compassion! Let all of the buried pain that you have repressed, out of a false sense of duty to keep a stiff upper lip, be unearthed and washed away in the cleansing, healing flow of My eternal love for you, right now. It is a matter of trust, My child. Will you trust Me with your pain today?

And Jesus went throughout all the cities and villages, teaching in their synagogues and proclaiming the gospel of the kingdom and healing every disease and every affliction (Matthew 9:35).

184

I AM STILL THE KING

Making a decision to do a thing, or not do it, will be made easier if you will really check your own heart. I have planted desires deep within you that I wish to bring into fruition. The reality is that many times, fear of displeasing others will crowd out your sensitivity to My voice. So I want you to first deal with your head knowledge and your fear, and then you will be able to see clearly how My Spirit is leading you. Just take the time to be quiet, and let Me show you what is blocking you from the truth. For it is not weighing the pros and cons of a matter, but discerning what is My will in any issue that is the principle thing. When your priorities are in order, everything else will also come into line. It is great wisdom to seek first and foremost My kingdom and My righteousness, and then everything else in your life will fall into its proper place. Now remember that I am still the King of My kingdom.

But seek first the kingdom of God and His righteousness, and all these things will be added to you (Matthew 6:33).

THE RIGHT DIRECTION

The road that you are traveling upon is the high-way to heaven; however, the road sign says that it is becoming narrower just up ahead. For broad is the path of destruction, and narrow is the way that leads to heaven. In My kingdom right now, rich young rulers on earth will sell all that they possess and give it to the poor, and then they will experience heaven-on-earth because they are following Me in freedom without any excess baggage. Trust Me now, little one, to show you what to eliminate from your life. Let Me reveal to you what is truly necessary and what is excess. As you let Me lighten the load you are carrying, you will begin to experience true freedom in every area of your life. So rejoice and be exceedingly glad that I have chosen this path for you. Because I love you, I want you to fully experience My plan for your life! You are headed in the right direction so relax and enjoy the scenery as we travel life's highway together today.

So now faith, hope, and love abide, these three; but the greatest of these is love (1 Corinthians 13:13).

COME FLY WITH ME

The gift of trust that I have placed within your heart is to be exercised continually, yet it is always a matter of your own choice to do so. You control the amount and the quality of your own individual desire to trust Me. You can always ask Me to help you to fully put your trust in Me, and I will be blessed to give you all of the help you will ever need. You can also seek for Me to deepen your level of trust in Me, and I will be delighted to take you deeper into My love. Cast the whole of your care now upon Me, and let Me lead you out into the promised land. Just take My hand like a little child, and totally abandon yourself to Me. You will not be disappointed! I can tell you that there are pleasures here at My right hand; they are more than enough to delight you forever and ever more. Are you ready to throw caution to the wind and really live your life to the fullest? If so, then come fly with Me today into the adventure of a lifetime.

Ah, Lord God! It is You who have made the heavens and the earth by Your great power and by Your outstretched arm! Nothing is too hard for You (Jeremiah 32:17).

SEED OF LOVE

Now is the time to worship Me in Spirit and in Truth. So set everything else aside for awhile, and simply come with all of your heart before My throne. I will show you how, with all of your being, to really enter into My presence. Just come to Me, presenting all that you are and all that you are not. Rest assured that I AM well able to take your sacrificial offering of self and translate it into a sweet-smelling fragrance of your love and devotion to Me. I savor the aroma of your worshiping adoration; it is as the sweetest of incense to My nostrils. I delight to breathe in your heartfelt love offerings, and I want you to know that your sacrifices of obedience do bring great pleasure to My heart. I know that you desire a closer, deeper, more intimate relationship with Me, as that desire in your heart was planted there by My very own hand. This seed of love is now springing up to blossom into bridal passion.

For by grace you have been saved through faith. And this is not your doing; it is the gift of God, not a result of works, so that no one may boast (Ephesians 2:8-9).

188

MY PERSONAL CARE

Trust Me now, little one, to have your best and highest interest at heart. By My death, I have provided everything you could ever need as an inheritance for you to receive. By My resurrection, I have given you power to embrace all of your inheritance and to enjoy it to the uttermost. Nothing has been left out; even every little detail was pre-arranged and is now being administered by My messengers. So come boldly before My throne of grace, and receive freely of My mercy and love for you. Just rest here now in the safety of My loving arms. Let all of your wants, concerns, and injuries be surrendered unto My personal care today. Watch with great expectancy to receive from My hand everything that you could ever need or desire beyond your wildest dreams, highest hopes, and greatest expectations! My love is all encompassing, and I am enfolding you right now in My most tender embrace. Can you feel it?

May you be strengthened with all power, according to His glorious might, for all endurance and patience with joy, giving thanks to the Father, who has qualified you to share in the inheritance of the saints in light (Colossians 1:11-12).

DIVINE REJUVENATION

When you are tired, it is not a sin to rest. I have created sleep as a time of divine rejuvenation. Remember My song to David of how I gave to My beloved sleep? It also means that I give to My beloved in their sleep! The night covers the earth like a blanket, yet the moon is there as a soft nightlight to glow in reflection of the sun and to let you know that daylight will soon come again since I have created both night and day. So do not fight the times that you may need extra rest, and see it as a time to draw closer to Me. As your subconscious mind is being renewed and healed, you will soon have the energy to resume your appointed tasks. Treasure each moment with Me, whether awake or asleep, knowing that I will never leave you nor forsake you. You can put your confidence fully in Me for I am trustworthy and you can trust Me completely with all of your life. I want you to really know that night and day are both the same to Me, and both were made for your pleasure because I love you.

When he calls to Me, I will answer him; I will be with him in trouble; I will rescue him and honor him. With long life I will satisfy him and show him My salvation (Psalm 91:15-16).

LET YOUR PRAISE RISE TO ME

Praise Me with your whole heart today, and watch as I reveal Myself to you in a more tangible manner. This exercise of your will to be obedient to My wishes is the door out into the supernatural realm of My domain. Praise is a release of the heart's emotion as well as an act of your obedient will. So do not wait for a feeling to rise up within you in order to praise Me. It is not that I am egocentric and need your uplifting, it is for your benefit that I ask you to do this. It not only lifts up your eyes to see My glory, it also is a channel for you to be able to receive exactly what you ask of Me. So when you want to see My healing manifest, begin to praise Me for this attribute of mine, and see that I will open the windows of heaven and pour out upon you My healing and divine health. I am your healer and the lifter of your head, so let your praise rise to me as incense from the throne of your heart where I reside. Let your lips rejoice in joyful praise of Who I Am, and expect to see Me move on your behalf today!

The Lord is my rock and my fortress and my deliverer, my God, my rock, in whom I take refuge, my shield, the horn of my salvation, my stronghold. I call upon the Lord, who is worthy to be praised, and I am saved from my enemies (Psalm 18:2-3).

MY MERCIFUL FORGIVENESS

Repentance brings with it a clean sweep of all of the things that cause pain and anguish of heart, mind, body, and soul. As you turn away from everything that has caused division in My family, others will follow suit. You can repent in spirit for another and help them by paving the way out of bondage with your tears and prayers, yet you must allow each person to exercise their own free will. So when you have done your part and feel satisfied that I have heard your heart's cry on behalf of others, please do not torment yourself further by holding on to that care, nursing it along as the occasion arises. No, on the contrary, throw it. Violently cast the whole of your concern, once and for all times, directly upon My capable shoulders, for this is the purpose that I came to undertake. I not only died to take away your sins, as well as those of the whole earth, I have hurled them into the sea of My own forgetfulness, the very ocean of My merciful forgiveness. Moreover, as I arose that third morning, your eternal place with Me was secured. We are alive, we are free, and we are one!

In Him we have redemption through His blood, the forgiveness of our trespasses, according to the riches of His grace, which He lavished upon us, in all wisdom and insight (Ephesians 1:7-8).

192

BLESSED JOURNEY

Your life will unfold like a beautiful flower as you continue to follow Me. My path is not hard but it is narrow. My yoke is easy and My burden is light, but it is not frivolous. I have a wonderful plan for your life with many exiting adventures to keep your mind and heart alert and overjoyed. Trust Me for what you cannot see up ahead; when it is the right time, all will be revealed. Too much information would only confuse and over burden you. I have a system, and everything is progressing nicely. You are headed in the right direction, and My Spirit is instructing you at every turn. So relax and enjoy this blessed journey with Me. Let Me make all of the difficult decisions for you. Let Me be your manager and your guide. I still have your very best interest at heart, and I really do delight to escort you along this eternal pathway of LIFE. Will you allow Me to be all that you will need today?

But the hour is coming, and it is now here, when the true worshipers will worship the Father in spirit and truth, for the Father is seeking such people to worship Him (John 4:23).

EVEN GREATER MEASURE

I have created you to be Mine! Not just to do things for Me or others, but, in reality, to be completely Mine so that every area of your life would sing out of your love for Me continually, and that we would walk hand in hand all across the face of the earth, and fly together all over heaven. Then our Oneness, which is the highest form of love possible, will be known by all those who see us, irresistibly drawing all those who hunger and thirst for true righteousness. As you allow your love for Me, because of My love for you, to be a witness to others, it will enlighten their path to Me, and many will be touched, healed, and delivered. They will be set free to be who I created them to be just by being around you. My power is eternally the same, but now I am releasing it in an even greater measure through you to meet the needs of those who are hungry. It is My anointing that will break the yokes of bondage in your midst.

For I am not ashamed of the gospel, for it is the power of God for salvation to everyone who believes, to the Jew first and also to the Greek. For in it the righteousness of God is revealed from faith for faith, as it is written, "The righteous shall live by faith" (Romans 1:16-17).

RISE UP!

It is never too late to rise up and begin again. As long as there is life in your heart and breath in your body, you can start over in a new direction. It may even be the same direction with a new attitude, but hope is the key word here. You must receive a new dose of this life-invigorating blessing from Me in order for you to be able to fully wrap your faith around it, and then you will be able to anchor yourself to My most holy will for your life. It is not what you have that counts in the long run, but it is what you do with what you have; first, by receiving everything that is given to you with gratitude. The deeper the sense of thanksgiving, the more freedom you will possess to use for My glory. By first enjoying it yourself, then you will truly be able to share it with others. Freely you have received so freely give! Now rise up in your most holy faith, and begin to rejoice in all of the good things that I have given to you just because I love you. So now, today, rise up!

And the Lord said, "If you had faith like a grain of mustard seed, you could say to this mulberry tree, 'be uprooted and planted in the sea,' and it would obey you" (Luke 17:6).

LOOK FORWARD

Treasure every moment of every day spent here in My presence. I have come to do you good and to be your Light-Guide through to the other side. Take off your shoes in recognition of My holy presence here with you right now, and shake loose all distracting spirits that were sent by hell to torment you. Release yourself from any confusion and all depression by calling upon My name in true reverence. Rise up, and take back what belongs to you! Just knowing that I have purchased it all for you by means of My own blood will give you all of the authority that you will ever need. Trust Me as you are placing one foot in front of the other here on My Holy Highway, and watch how I will direct your life in an ever-increasing splendor of MY knowledge and grace. It is time now for you to trust Me in every area of your life, and to know that I am well pleased with you. As we look forward to a new beginning together, you will be able to say goodbye to the past and not look back.

So then, as we have opportunity, let us do good to everyone, and especially to those who are of the household of faith (Galatians 6:10).

YOU MUST TURN YOUR BACK ON WHAT WAS

OR MIGHT HAVE BEEN

IN ORDER TO FULLY EMBRACE

WHAT IS AND WHAT IS TO COME!

About the author

Suzannah has been walking with the Lord since 1973. She is the wife of Russell, a retired U.S. Army soldier. His duty stations led them to many places in the world, and she had often referred to themselves as "United States Government Missionaries." One of their travels led them to Germany where they were Pastors for many years of "Heaven Bound Ministries." They also held local meetings in German churches as well as "After Glow" services in the Army Chapels. She has been listening to the Lord's voice since that time and writing down what He has spoken to her. In this endeavor, she has compiled over twelve hand-written books and is now publishing this one to share some of the Lord's blessings with you.

Suzannah has made it her lifestyle to enjoy a quiet time of going before the Lord and asking Him for His message for the day. This book, and books to come, are a result of that time of listening to and writing the Lord's messages. Suzannah is highly prophetic and loves to worship our Lord with her beautiful and colorful handmade flags. In addition to being prophetic and keenly attuned to hearing The Lord's voice daily, she has also received degrees in Christian Counseling, served as Area board Vice Presidents of Retreats, Ministries, Outreach, for "Women's Aglow Fellowship International," and assisted Russell when he was Director of the "Orange County Rescue Center" Thrift Store in Santa Ana, California.

Suzannah now desires that these "Words from the Lord" she is offering to you here be received as a blessing of love and encouragement. Please be in expectation as we have seen our MOST HIGH GOD manifest HIMSELF in many mighty and surprising ways through her ministry. The Fitzroy's have three wonderful daughters, all of whom are in Christian ministry in both California and New Mexico where they now reside, as well as in the QUANTUM TIME ZONE of the LORD!

To contact the author send email to:
REJOICEspotmosthigh@gmail.com

T.R.U.S.T.

- True

  - Revelation

    - Unleashes

      - Spiritual

        - Tenacity

THOSE WHO LOVE YOUR INSTRUCTION HAVE GREAT PEACE AND DO NOT STUMBLE
(Psalm 119:165 NLT)

To order more copies of
REJOICE The Lord is Our Keeper
send email to

REJOICEspotmosthigh@gmail.com

REJOICE The Lord is Our Keeper
is also available at:
The store at XPmedia.com
Amazon.com and other online bookstores
Christian bookstores

For wholesale purchases, please contact:
usaresource@xpmedia.com or
Anchordistributors.com

CSA
PUBLISHING

XPPublishing.com
A ministry of XP Ministries